M000073614

INDUSTRIAL
IS WHAT WE DO

INDUSTRIAL
IS WHAT WE DO

Building Wisconsin's Future
on a Foundation of Industry

JEFF HOFFMAN

HOUNDSTOOTH
PRESS

INDUSTRIAL IS WHAT WE DO

Building Wisconsin's Future on a Foundation of Industry

ISBN	978-1-5445-3281-3	*Hardcover*
	978-1-5445-3280-6	*Paperback*
	978-1-5445-3279-0	*Ebook*

CONTENTS

HELP WANTED

WISCONSIN HAS A PROBLEM. A people problem.

A lot of strange things came out of COVID-19, things that went beyond a public health crisis. The Great Resignation—the movement of millions of Americans not coming back to their jobs—stands out at the top of my list. As you slowly ventured back into the world in the summer of 2020 to support local businesses, it might have occurred to you that we need more people. You might have been visiting your favorite restaurant and waited over an hour to get served because of a lack of wait-staff. Perhaps you spent an additional fifteen minutes in line to get your groceries because six checkout clerks were reduced to three. You tried finding childcare as you went back to work, only to discover your daycare provider was shut down because its help was nowhere to be found. Services that you took for granted prepandemic suddenly became hard to find and even harder to schedule. Where did all the workers go?

While many were caught off guard by people's sudden lack of interest in showing up for work, industrial companies around the state were not. They had already been dealing with a vanishing workforce for several years leading up to the pandemic.

How did we get to this point? As the saying goes, demographics are your destiny. The state of Wisconsin simply does not have enough people to keep up. Our state is aging; a wave of retirements is hitting our workforce, and we currently do not have access to the depth of people needed to replace the legacy knowledge and skill sets developed over almost two centuries of making things. To further complicate matters, Wisconsin's successful baby boomers are heading south for the winter. And perhaps most importantly, millennials and Gen Z generally have not shown interest in working in the industries that made Wisconsin.

For the better part of the past decade, business and economic development organizations across the state have been banging the drum about this looming demographic time bomb. Now that time has arrived. The coming decade will be one of the fastest transformational periods that industry has ever encountered. Wisconsin has choices to make regarding how we stem the tide of population stagnation and loss of the traditional blue-collar workforce. If we do nothing, our industrial employers will be forced to expand in other regions. Wisconsin will not even have enough people to replace its retirees, let alone to provide the additional workers needed to grow a business. We are facing an existential threat to our economic future.

As the Great Resignation accelerated throughout 2021, I recognized we finally had a chance to conquer our greatest challenge. The lack of people was no longer an isolated problem that only impacted industry. It had become a pervasive problem that was impacting every walk of life and every business. When *everyone* is impacted, change can happen and happen fast. And in my opinion, it can't happen fast enough.

I believe an economic renaissance in the state of Wisconsin is on the horizon—that is, *if* we can provide our existing industrial companies with the firepower they will need to make the transition over the coming decade. While we face many challenges, they are not insurmountable. Nearly all states across the country, especially those in the upper Midwest, are confronting the exact same problems that we are facing. I have talked to some of the best minds in business throughout the state of Wisconsin, and I believe the strengths of our people can lead us to the solutions we need. We are not talking about blowing up the system as we know it and starting over. Like most businesses with history, a story to tell, and a product to sell, the state of Wisconsin does not need to start from scratch.

FORWARD: THE MOTTO OF WISCONSIN

Wisconsin's state motto is "Forward," reflecting the state's continuous drive to be a national leader. I proudly admit that I am a Wisconsin lifer. I was born and raised in Port Washington, a town of ten thousand people located on the shores of Lake Michigan with the iconic St. Mary's Church on the hill. Our claim to fame is Fish Day, the self-proclaimed World's Largest One-Day Outdoor Fish Fry. Does it get more Wisconsin than that?

For my college experience, I ventured to the community of Whitewater, a town similar in size to Port, but only when you include the population of the student body. University of Wisconsin (UW)-Whitewater is the largest business school in the state; however, don't let that title fool you. UW-Whitewater is the classic Wisconsin small town located in the middle of rural America. When you visit Whitewater for the first time, your first question will likely be: how in the heck did a university ever decide to locate here?

While at UW-Whitewater, I was very lucky to find my calling, a career in industrial real estate.

Upon graduating in 2000, I relocated to Waukesha County, where I have resided ever since. My role as the cochair of the industrial real estate practice for one of Wisconsin's oldest commercial real estate firms places me at the center of economic development decisions for companies, developers, and communities. Over the course of a twenty-one-year career, I have brokered more than $1.3 billion in industrial real estate deals for Wisconsin-based companies and developers, and understanding what drives their investment decisions is my responsibility.

In my fifth year in business, I experienced the good fortune of participating in the Leadership Waukesha program. The opportunity served as a springboard into one of my true passions, economic development—specifically, exploring how public policy influences economic development, both positively and negatively. Elected office, especially at the local level, is generally a thankless position. It mostly involves volunteer hours late into the evening, and much of the feedback received comes from constituents who are fired up about something that is bothering them. While national elections capture the headlines and dominate the news cycle, it is local and state governments that make many of the decisions that actually impact our day-to-day lives.

Through my passion, I have had the opportunity to participate in leadership roles for several business associations that focus on improving the business climate in the state of Wisconsin. Some of my key positions have included board chair and public policy chair of the Waukesha County Business Alliance (WCBA), board chair of the Commercial Association of Realtors Wisconsin (CARW), public policy chair of the National Association of Industrial and Office Parks (NAIOP) - Wisconsin Chapter, executive committee of the Wisconsin Realtors Association (WRA), and board chair of the Independent Business Association of Wisconsin (IBAW). My experience in these associations allowed me to participate in countless business roundtables and industry events in which business owners and executives plan for Wisconsin's economic future.

Throughout this book, I will cover many of the competitive advantages that Wisconsin already possesses. The quality of the people who live here, because of their work ethic and loyalty, is often cited as one of the best features of growing a business in Wisconsin. We make things in Wisconsin and have for decades. Milwaukee was known as the Machine Shop of the World for the better part of the twentieth century. Sure, you can go to other areas of the country and try to build a new workforce, but when you speak to companies that have done so, you'll hear the common refrain, "We just couldn't find the work ethic of the average Wisconsinite."

While we have great people, we do not have enough of them. The monumental challenge of simply *finding* people continues to be cited as the number one problem facing the business community. And yet, in the past decade, we've made very little progress toward making long-term plans that articulate specific goals and metrics for how to change course. Reciting our deficiencies in an echo chamber leads to paralysis in decision-making and, ultimately, an acceptance of the reality we live in. Simply talking about the big problem is no longer good enough.

State business climates are traditionally ranked on taxes and regulatory environments. Less in both categories is more. When I started my business career, Wisconsin was viewed as a high-tax, heavily regulated, unionized state. If you asked any business executive what was holding them back from investing in Wisconsin back then, I almost guarantee that you'd hear one of those three answers. These challenges are rarely discussed as front-burner issues in 2022. Growing our workforce and the population of the state is what keeps business owners up at night these days. The elephant in the room is that the labor shortages we all face will get worse before they get better. Especially in the bread-and-butter area of Wisconsin's industrial economy. The task forces, roundtables, and general airing-of-grievances sessions that have consumed much of the time of the private sector to date need to transition into a plan of action to produce tangible results. We need to create specific goals and educate our local and state policy leaders on how we can collectively get the job done. This is not a job to hand off. The private sector has just as much responsibility as the public sector in delivering the solutions we need to move the state forward.

TWO PATHS. ONE FUTURE.

When a problem is big, and this one certainly is, we have a tendency to get bogged down in the fantasy of trying to solve everything at once. The "everything is on the table" approach leads to being overwhelmed and, ultimately, a failure to prioritize the most pressing issues. Ever since we emerged from the Great Recession, we could see a not-too-distant future in which the cupboard of talent would become barren as the legacy blue-collar workforce of Wisconsin aged and headed toward retirement. A talent shortage is like compounding interest on a credit card. It doesn't bite you immediately, but run the deficit for an extended period and you'll be sitting at the bottom of a deep hole without a ladder. Imagine the Green Bay Packers having to forfeit three of their midround draft picks on an annual basis over a five-year period. The current team could compete over the short term, but by year five the talent gap between them and the rest of the league would be obvious. As the postpandemic economy has roared back, many of our employers are operating without their annual allotment of draft picks, and they cannot keep up.

The fork in the road is upon us. Times are changing and our competitive advantage is eroding. If we do not adapt, we will be forced to accept the bleak future that comes with fewer people and fewer opportunities. We are trying to keep up, but we lack the horsepower. Regions like the Southeast, from the Carolinas to Texas, and the Southwest states of Arizona and Nevada have become the darlings of the site selection community for manufacturing projects. Their offerings are simple yet effective: business- and weather-friendly climates, lower taxes and regulations, and growing populations.

There needs to be a better way. And I believe there is. In my opinion, Wisconsin has tried to distance itself from its industrial heritage. Many buy into the idea that the Rust Belt economy that helped build our state has long passed us by and we need to quickly adapt and excel in new industry to change the tide. To be clear, there is absolutely a place for the "new" economy in the future of Wisconsin. Hitting a home run with a massive tech company success could completely change the trajectory of the state. But I think going all in on the startup lottery is better suited for other areas of the country. That doesn't fit our style. We grind, we persevere, we produce, and we do it over and over again. We can solve the problems facing our industrial companies the same way. Before we turn our back on our industrial heritage, perhaps it's time to recognize that we have a built-in competitive advantage we might be taking for granted: our existing industrial companies. Many of these companies are at the forefront of the technological revolution that is delivering the era of Industry 4.0, a generation of industry that will unleash the exponential powers of man teaming with machines.

My intent for this book is to create a path of action that can position Wisconsin's industrial economy to thrive over the coming decade—a time frame I believe will be known as the Decade of Industrial. A time frame in which America will experience the reshoring of manufacturing, the relocation of supply chains needed to service local markets, and the consumer purchasing of more and more goods through e-commerce fulfillment centers. Much of what I cover is related to public policies that could be impactful in helping with this mission. First and foremost, I answer the question: how do we provide the workforce needed to win the Decade of Industrial?

This book lays out a handful of impactful solutions for the public and private sectors that are both actionable and measurable. We review the existing state of Wisconsin's industrial workforce and how we can grow it. We dive deep into the strength of our technical college system. We look into the not-too-distant future in which man and machine will lead the way in delivering new growth opportunities. We discuss how to be a national leader in workforce housing. We examine the opportunities to deliver world-class infrastructure and the need for modern business parks. We also cover the keys to pulling it all together: building upon what we *already have* here in this state, building upon our unique competitive advantages, and leveraging our industrial strengths as a platform to change. We profile what the future of industry in Wisconsin looks like.

Before you can embrace creating solutions, gaining a proper perspective of our challenges is necessary. My oldest child, Gavin, started middle school this past year. My wife and I were both rather nervous as we sat in the introductory parent meeting to kick off the new school year. This was such a big step for our son. How could he possibly be ready for the responsibilities of middle school? One of his soon-to-be teachers opened the meeting by providing a sage piece of advice. We as parents need to focus on parenting our son to become the person we want him to be when he is thirty-five years old, not who we want him to be next week. This one comment provided the confidence and clarity my wife and I needed and changed much of our thought process just as we were about to start our new journey.

The current pace of change impacting the world of business does not allow for considering the twenty-year time frame of a child growing into an adult, but the concept is quite relevant. Having a proper perspective requires focusing on what we want the state of Wisconsin's industrial economy to look like in 2030, not next year. So how do we get there? We use our strengths as our foundation and get to work. We use our industrial strength. But before we dive into how we are going to create Wisconsin 2030, we must consider the future that almost was. The future known as Wisconn Valley.

CHAPTER 1

THE EAGLE HAS LANDED?

> "If you must play, decide upon three things at the start:
> the rules of the game, the stake, and the quitting time."
> —CHINESE PROVERB

THE YEAR 2020 WAS SUPPOSED to be the breakout year for the city of Milwaukee and the state of Wisconsin. All the stars were aligned. The Milwaukee Bucks were dazzling the NBA in the brand-new Fiserv Forum and possessed the best record in the league. Everyone believed the electric Fiserv Forum would host the NBA Finals in June and move straight into the Democratic National Convention (DNC) two weeks later. Two months after that, Whistling Straits was to host the prestigious Ryder Cup and provide the world a stunning glimpse of the fall canopy along Lake Michigan. On the economic development front, Taiwanese global manufacturing giant Foxconn was slated to open the first phase of Project Flying Eagle, its codename for what would be called Wisconn Valley, a massive Mount Pleasant campus known as the "Eighth Wonder of the World." This one-million-square-foot giga-factory was going to support thousands of new jobs with the production of ten-inch liquid crystal display (LCD) screens. Or would it be 5G networks? Or smart city prototypes? The specifics weren't nailed down, but one of those tech industries was going to happen. The year 2020 was supposed to be the year that we finally were going to tell the world that Wisconsin had arrived.

Then COVID-19 hit. The NBA abruptly stopped, and the Bucks were an early exit from the postponed playoffs held in the Disney bubble. The DNC was on again, off again, reduced scale, to no scale, and then to a virtual conference. The Ryder Cup was postponed to fall of 2021. And Foxconn? The company that was to reinvent high-tech manufacturing as we knew it? Foxconn delved into a public relations nightmare that ensnared both the company and the state of Wisconsin as 2020 came to a close. Wisconsin was on the cusp of its long-awaited breakout, and we missed it. Again.

MAKE AMERICA GREAT AGAIN

On November 8, 2016, a slim margin of ten thousand votes delivered the state of Wisconsin, and its ten electoral votes, to Donald Trump. I remember watching the results trickle in that evening. Trump had already won the key states of Florida and Ohio. Although Pennsylvania looked promising, the election was far from over. When Wisconsin was called, the enormity of what had just happened sunk in. Donald Trump was going to be elected the 45th President of the United States. The ultimate outsider had pulled off the unthinkable. Love him or hate him, Trump campaigned on the "Make America Great Again" slogan that, at its core, was a call to action to revive domestic manu-facturing. A key line from his inauguration speech on January 20, 2017, foretold the economic priorities that were to come from the administration: "One by one, the factories shuttered and left our shores, with not even a thought about the millions and millions of American workers that were left behind. The wealth of our middle class has been ripped from their homes and then redistributed all across the world."

The United States was once again going to be a global leader in manufacturing. Not only were we going to make things in America, but we were also going to entice foreign companies to make their products here as well. The Foxconn project was to be one of the signature economic development projects of Trump's "Make America Great Again" agenda.

Trump's journey to becoming president started in a crowded primary field of accomplished Republican governors, one being Governor Scott Walker of Wisconsin. A front-runner in the early stages of the summer of 2015, Walker was knocked on his heels by the Trump phenomenon and ultimately knocked out of the contest within months of Trump entering the fray. Walker was a relentless cheerleader for economic development. He launched his 2010 gubernatorial campaign with the big and bold promise of creating 250,000 new jobs during his first term. Walker and the Republican senate and assembly moved decisively to lower taxes and regulations as they came to power in 2011. They were able to achieve one of the most pro-business policy agendas across the United States; however, job growth was a grind. Wisconsin was consistently ranked in the bottom half of job growth in the country throughout Walker's tenure.

The state generated 129,000 new jobs during his first term and a total of 233,000 jobs by the end of his second term.[1] In championing policies such as the Manufacturing Tax Credit, which effectively eliminated state income taxes for manufacturers, Walker hitched his wagon to a boom in jobs led by old-line industrial companies, but the job growth merely trickled in. What was happening? Wisconsin was making progress, but at a snail's pace. Job creation in manufacturing had staggered through the prior decade, and the Great Recession knocked it on the mat. Wisconsin dropped 125,000 manufacturing jobs, *one in five*, since the beginning of 2000. But that is only half the story. Despite the pain of shedding 20 percent of its workforce, the manufacturing industry continued to increase output and grew by $3 billion in value over the same time frame.[2] We were still making a lot of things here, just with fewer people.

THE EAGLE CIRCLES WISCONSIN

When Project Flying Eagle appeared on Wisconsin's radar in spring of 2017, the opportunity immediately turned some heads in the development community. The project, an initial build-out of a one-million-square-foot high-tech manufacturing facility that would host more than one thousand employees, would be a home run for whichever state won the deal. This was the type of project Wisconsin never got a shot at. The rumors, speculation, and excitement were palpable. What other states were under consideration for the factory? What sites in Wisconsin could accommodate such a development? Where would we find the workers? Did we really have a shot at this? As June arrived, the *Wall Street Journal* officially announced Wisconsin as a surprise contender for what had grown into a projected $10 billion investment by the global giant Foxconn.[3]

As the usual suspects such as Ohio and Texas were announced as additional frontrunners, the conventional wisdom was that Wisconsin could never win the deal. Number one, securing a megaproject like the Foxconn development wasn't how the state traditionally grew its economy. We didn't offer enough incentives, taxes weren't low enough, regulations were too high...that's just not how we do things. Number two, the sheer scope of the updated project was well beyond anything Wisconsin could handle. In a matter of months, the initial projection of one thousand employees had exploded to the need for thirteen thousand! The concept of thirteen thousand employees operating from a newly constructed, high-tech ecosystem in Wisconsin, which would be known as Wisconn Valley, would have been deemed pure science fiction just months earlier.

But this was our big chance. Wisconsin needed to be all in for this one. The state was lagging its peers when it came to high-profile economic development wins, and our job creation numbers proved it. We weren't just losing; we weren't even invited to the dance. Something had to change, and change it did. Governor Walker reinvented the Wisconsin Economic Development Corporation (WEDC) over his prior six years as governor. The scattered Department of Commerce was taken apart, and a top-level team of professionals was assembled to transform the new agency. WEDC ramped up its national presence quickly. Wisconsin was no longer going to wait for economic development; we were going to put the state on the map of large corporate site selectors. With a revamped WEDC and pro-business policy reforms, the state was catapulting up the charts of national business rankings. But we still needed a signature project that would show the world we were no longer part of flyover country.

As the summer of 2017 advanced, I continued to marvel that Wisconsin was still in the Foxconn sweepstakes. How was this possible? Hints of political motivations were leaked. Was President Trump yielding influence with Foxconn Chairman Terry Gou as a payback to Wisconsin for delivering the election? Was the speaker of the house, Paul Ryan, twisting arms? Had former RNC head and new Trump chief of staff, Reince Priebus, pulled some strings? It didn't matter. Foxconn was at our doorstep, and they were going to deliver the new economy we had been searching for. With Foxconn as the state's partner, we were going to create Wisconn Valley, a global technology hub based in the Midwest. The LCD plant was merely the start. Visions of smart cities and cutting-edge 5G networks were suddenly part of the project. Even the reconstruction of I-94 was going to be master planned for dedicated, autonomous trucking lanes designed to help move the Foxconn supply chain. That supply chain was supposed to deliver an additional forty-four thousand jobs to the area.

The Walker administration proudly placed the "Wisconsin Is Open for Business" slogan on all of the state's welcome signs. Walker staked his claim as the Jobs Governor. Everything he had accomplished up to this date had prepared the state to compete and win Project Flying Eagle. On July 26, 2017, Wisconsin did the unthinkable. We won. Foxconn decided to build

Wisconn Valley here, and it was going to transform the state's economy in ten short years.

The Foxconn deal was signed with much fanfare on November 10, 2017, at SC Johnson, a historic Racine company. I attended the event, which included all the movers and shakers in the Wisconsin economic development circles who had participated in the pursuit. Governor Walker was front and center, Speaker of the House Paul Ryan was a guest of honor, and the man of the hour, Foxconn Chairman Terry Gou, flew in for the day to commemorate the deal with an official contract signing. The ceremony was the equivalent of the Academy Awards for the economic development community. Wisconsin, a Rust Belt manufacturing powerhouse, was no longer going to hemorrhage middle-class manufacturing jobs. We were going to create them right here and export our newfound prowess around the globe. That day almost felt like April 7, 1993, the day that Reggie White signed with the Green Bay Packers. The losing was going to stop right now. I remember the feeling that came over me, with my attention fixated on the stage. Chairman Gou was about to shake Governor Walker's hand to officially seal the deal. He was proudly wearing a Wisconn Valley hat as he confidently stood in front of the backdrop of American and Wisconsin flags. I beamed with a sense of pride. We were no longer the little exurb of Chicago!

From the get-go, the Foxconn announcement ignited a lightning rod of strong opinions, both for and against. The majority of the large business trade groups vocally supported the development. However, many of Walker's proudest supporters, small business owners of industrial companies, were not only perplexed by the decision to embrace the global giant but were also against it. More to come on that shortly. But despite the disagreement, Wisconsin finally had a trophy economic development project secured, the framework of the deal had been cut, and now it was time to execute. An economic development pursuit of this size is inevitably tied to an incentive offering from the winning state. Wisconsin offered Foxconn a package that was well outside Wisconsin's comfort zone: $4 billion (yes, billion, with a "b") of state and local dollars were placed on the table in the form of tax credits and tax increment financing (TIF).

After the contract signing, the project was supposed to move at warp speed. A massive four-thousand-acre tract of land in Mount Pleasant, located on the southern end of Racine County, was targeted for the multiple phases of the development. The site was bound by I-94 to the west and Racine and Lake Michigan to the east. Milwaukee was twenty-five minutes to the north and Chicago was forty-five minutes to the south. In addition to being in an excellent location, the area had relatively flat topography with limited wetlands and environmental corridors. It was one of those sites I frequently drove past on my way to Chicago and wondered: why is nothing being built here? The simple answer was there was no infrastructure. The utility and infrastructure upgrades needed for this area could not be justified without a massive project to kick-start it. We were talking about a full buildout of brand-new sewer and water service, electrical grid, and roads. Just the necessary infrastructure upgrades approached a half billion dollars. Add on the acquisition of all the land at $50,000 per acre, and the

Village of Mount Pleasant had effectively agreed to finance a $1 billion TIF district. That sum would be far and away the largest local economic development project undertaken in the history of the state of Wisconsin. And unlike the tax credits offered by the state, the $1 billion was an immediate thirty-year liability not contingent upon job creation. Welcome to the economic development big leagues. *Gulp...*

THE EAGLE MISSES THE LANDING

Unfortunately, 2018 did not go so well for the advancement of Wisconn Valley or Governor Walker. The economics of manufacturing ten-inch LED screens in the United States came under more and more scrutiny. The numbers didn't add up, even with the potential of $3 billion in tax credit incentives. The months passed with no signs of the one-million-square-foot plant. Nothing more than ongoing site grading and delivery of infrastructure around the six square miles of the project boundaries was happening.

Additionally, the politics of the deal had gone completely off the tracks. The signature economic development project of Governor Walker, possibly the most pro-business governor the state had ever experienced, became a massive liability in the 2018 governor's race. Not only did Democrats not like the deal, but one of Walker's key constituency groups did not either. Small- to medium-sized industrial businesses were concerned. Very concerned. With unemployment hovering around 3 percent and local businesses screaming for job applicants, how could Wisconsin possibly sell the farm to a foreign company that was promising thirteen thousand newly created jobs, which consultants suggested could expand to more than fifty thousand jobs once the supply chain was built out? That was more than half the size of the entire city of Racine. Where would these people come from? And why were we shelling out $3 billion in tax credits to a company that didn't even know where Wisconsin was two years ago? Tony Evers, the unassuming head of the Department of Public Instruction, upset Governor Walker in the November 2018 election, with Foxconn providing a key wedge issue in the campaign. Foxconn had become daily media fodder. We were promised billions of dollars in capital spending and thousands of people employed in high-tech jobs, but it wasn't happening—at least nowhere near the pace that was promised on November 10, 2017.

Fast-forward to December 2018, a little more than one year since the surreal deal signing at SC Johnson. Wisconsin Manufacturers & Commerce (WMC) held its annual Business Day in Madison event at Monona Terrace. The event typically brings in north of five hundred leading business executives and economic development professionals from around the state, who come to hear from industry experts on how we can grow the state's economy. The keynote speaker that day was then Foxconn Wisconsin lead Alan Yeung, making one of the first public appearances from the company in several months.

Hosted a little more than a month after Walker was defeated, the WMC event promised suspense and potential drama. What was to become of Walker's signature deal? Would Foxconn pull out? Or would it be "on with the show"? The stage was set for Yeung, a UW-Madison graduate and accomplished executive within Foxconn. He gave an hour-long presentation in which he firmly committed that Wisconn Valley was not only going to happen, but it was also going to change the world. He convincingly painted the picture of what the future was going to hold: smart cities, artificial intelligence, autonomous vehicles, and 5G networks. Foxconn was going to change, shape, and dominate all these new industries right here in Wisconsin.

As the hour-long presentation continued, I began to realize that there was little substance being offered. The presentation had the feel of a TEDx Talk on steroids. The first phase of the project was supposed to be breaking ground in spring of 2019, only four months away. Yeung made no mention of how the campus design was advancing, no mention of facility details, no mention of what the first wave of hiring was going to look like. Nothing. The transformational development that was to turn Wisconsin into a global leader within Industry 4.0 became a high-level pitch deck of aspirational goals with zero guidance on plans for execution. As Yeung concluded his presentation, it was obvious that Foxconn was not breaking ground in the spring of 2019. It was also obvious there was substance to the rumors swirling around the project. The entire project was in jeopardy.

The year of 2019 passed with fits and starts for the project. Bill Mitchell, a Foxconn VP and the local project figurehead for a period of time, said it best in early 2019: "We're flying the airplane and we're designing and building it as we go." The largest economic development deal in the history of Wisconsin, with a $4 billion incentive package passed eighteen months prior, now had a key executive stating they were building it as they went?

For better or worse, Wisconsin was all in on what seemed to be more like a speculative venture capital investment than a generational economic hub.

Finally, on August 19, 2019, Foxconn broke ground on the first phase of the one-million-square-foot fabrication plant. Additionally, it kick-started a 277,000-square-foot technology center and an eclectic, globe-shaped building that would house its internet and server businesses. The project was moving, but questions remained. What was Foxconn actually making? How many jobs would be created? The answers seemed to change on a weekly basis. A lot of companies use stealth in their business planning and strategies, but something was not adding up. That large of a manufacturing plant requires a supply chain. Supply chains cannot start overnight, and many in the real estate community believed that once the main plant construction started, the supply chain would start securing positions in the local market. But it was quiet. Dead quiet.

COVID-19 couldn't have come at a worse time for the Foxconn project. About halfway into the construction of the first series of buildings, the pandemic shut down the global economy and scrambled supply chains. Foxconn was set to deliver $450 million worth of facilities, but the jobs were nowhere to be found. As 2020 ended, WEDC notified Foxconn that they were ineligible for their annual tax credit award due to their failure to secure minimum hiring milestones. While the public airing of mutual grievances felt acrimonious, there was a general sense that both parties understood the writing on the wall. The aspirational new economy of Wisconn Valley was no longer going to happen, and the public seemingly had moved on. While the $4 billion incentive package was jaw dropping, 75 percent of the award ($3 billion) had been negotiated as contingent tax credits. Foxconn didn't create the jobs, and so they did not receive the tax credits. The structure of the contingent incentive agreement was ultimately a saving grace for both the state and the company.

THE EAGLE FLIES THE COOP

The year 2021 saw Foxconn deliver nearly 1.5 million square feet of facilities, but the uses of the new plants appeared to have strayed far from the projected vision. Foxconn was reverting to its roots in contract manufacturing, evidenced by announcements such as a short-term COVID-related contract that would produce ten thousand respirators for Medtronic.[4] An additional buzz swirled about the chance to produce electric vehicles for Fisker on the Mount Pleasant campus, but an opportunity emerged for Foxconn to buy a stake in Lordstown Motors, an existing Ohio electric vehicle company with a 6.2-million-square-foot automotive plant. Foxconn ultimately decided to move forward with the Lordstown opportunity, and Wisconsin once again missed out on the promises of Wisconn Valley. The unrealistic goals of the original deal had to be reset for both parties. On April 20, 2021, Governor Evers announced that the state had successfully come to terms with Foxconn on a renegotiated contract. The job creation goal was cut by 90 *percent*. That's 13,000 jobs down to 1,454. Foxconn is here, but the future success of Wisconn Valley will likely be written by companies other than Foxconn.

The $1 billion of infrastructure investments placed in Mount Pleasant will ultimately drive a large net benefit to southeast Wisconsin. The proximity of the site to Chicago is simply too good of a location to not attract an alternative development. As we regroup and transition to what comes next, we also need to take advantage of the opportunity to debrief and answer some critical questions as to what the heck happened. Like many business and political leaders, I personally supported the Foxconn development when it was announced. It was big and bold. It was exactly what many of us thought the state needed. It is also necessary to acknowledge that if we knew then what we know now, this project certainly would not have received the political support for a fast-tracked approval process and a $4 billion incentive package. My individual debrief of the Foxconn saga focuses on three crucial lessons:

- Had the Foxconn development scaled as projected, the stresses placed on the labor pool would have been virtually impossible to navigate for the surrounding area employers based on current demographic trends coupled with the existing housing stock needed to support the job growth.

- Wisconsin possesses the tools to play and win in the economic development big leagues. Yes, the incentive package is what drives the headlines, but we also have access to a workforce with a great reputation, a highly dependable utility grid, abundant fresh water, and an ample supply of well-located land required for development.

- You cannot simply wish into existence an entire "new economy" or a cluster of market-leading companies overnight. Even with $4 billion thrown at it. Economic development that supports a cluster of market-leading companies occurs organically. One shining light attracts another. We need to find the shining lights in the state and work hard to grow them here. If we build the foundation, a sustainable ecosystem can scale to great heights.

And now, time to turn the page. We can learn many great lessons from Foxconn, and to understand what we need to do differently in the future, we need to examine the strength of our roots.

CHAPTER 2

GROW OUR OWN

"You win games with your strengths, not your weaknesses."
—BEAR BRYANT

"IF MILWAUKEE WAS LOCATED on the shores of Lake Superior, we would call it Lake Inferior." Rich Meeusen, the CEO of Badger Meter from 2002 to 2018, often repeated this remark at business events. The statement bluntly tells of the average Wisconsinite's struggles with bragging. We are not raised to seek out front-page headlines. We get our jobs done quietly and competently. Work hard, play hard. Rinse and repeat. Our humble roots often detract from our ability to confidently sell the amenities and lifestyle that we can deliver to businesses and residents who choose to grow in Wisconsin.

Meeusen was one of my favorite business leaders in the Milwaukee area. He was a CPA by training, but if you got him rolling with a mic in his hand, you might think he was auditioning for a role at the local comedy club. Unique to the world of Wisconsin CEOs, he embraced the bully pulpit, and he told it how it was. The good, the bad, and the ugly. Rich wanted to get the Milwaukee area to think broader and bigger, and he was not afraid of his critics. The leadership he provided during his tenure was not only incredibly successful for Badger Meter, but it also proved that a CEO could provide great influence in the community outside the confines of his or her company. Rich was an instrumental figure in the creation of the Water Council, which set out in 2007 to build the Silicon Valley of Fresh Water right here in Milwaukee. Rich and fellow founders uncovered a competitive edge that the state of Wisconsin had hiding in plain sight: over one hundred legacy manufacturing companies that possessed expertise in manufacturing products and creating processes that impacted the delivery of fresh water, the most important commodity on the face of the planet, essential for life. The Water Council was the platform that would sing from the rooftops that Milwaukee possessed a global-leading cluster of industry, and we wanted more. Finally, we had a cheerleader.

We make things in Wisconsin. As mentioned in the introduction, Milwaukee was known as "The Machine Shop of the World" throughout the twentieth century. An economy dependent on manufacturing might seem boring, but it also brings great security. The state has a large concentration of small- to medium-sized privately held businesses that have traditionally grown through private funding and grit. Scrappiness aligns with our personality and identity as a state. A large part of the private sector backlash against the Foxconn deal was the perception that the state opened its coffers to a company that had no history within or ties to Wisconsin. We grow our own talent, and we grow our own companies. As Meeusen's "Lake Inferior" comment implies, one of our biggest challenges is telling the outside world exactly *what* we make.

Many of our homegrown businesses quietly advance the development of leading-edge technologies within their industries. They continue to expand revenue, jobs, and supply chains, all of which builds communities. While currently fitting better into the category of bigger businesses, Milwaukee Tool and Generac are great examples of legacy Milwaukee-area companies that redefined themselves over the past decade and are exploding with new growth opportunities.

MILWAUKEE DOES IT BETTER

Milwaukee Tool has dominated business headlines over the past several years. They are the largest supplier of power hand tools in North America, and their rapid expansion is showing no sign of letting up. They closed out last year as an industry Goliath, but when you stop and take a closer look at the timeline in which they have accelerated, the story is even more amazing.

Only a decade ago, Milwaukee Tool had roughly three hundred employees and $400 million in top-line revenue. Fast-forward to the end of 2021, and their regional head count is up to an astonishing 3,500 employees and total revenue of *$8 billion*! And they believe much more runway is to come. Consider the significant real estate commitments in the Milwaukee area that Milwaukee Tool announced in 2021 alone:[5]

- Acquired a 377,000-square-foot office tower in downtown Milwaukee that will house two thousand employees.

- Constructing a 215,000-square-foot R & D center in Menomonee Falls.

- Leased a 395,000-square-foot warehouse in Menomonee Falls.

- Moved into a 52,000-square-foot office building in Menomonee Falls.

- Opened a 75,000-square-foot manufacturing plant in West Bend.

Founded in 1924, Milwaukee Tool will soon celebrate its centennial anniversary in the state of Wisconsin. It presents an excellent example of how the Wisconsin industrial economy can lead the way: take an existing product and simply make it, market it, and service it better than the competition. Hand tools have been around for decades, and competitors like Stanley Black & Decker and Makita have similar product lines. Milwaukee Tool is simply out-executing the competition and taking market share.

GENERAC POWERS THROUGH

Generac is another Wisconsin success story. Founded by entrepreneur Robert Kern in 1959 out of his barn in Wales, Wisconsin, it is now recognized as the number one manufacturer of home backup generators and has a market cap closing in on $30 billion. Much like Milwaukee Tool, Generac experienced much of its exponential growth over the past decade with an explosive phase beginning in 2019.

How did Generac go from a quiet company located in the middle of Waukesha County to a darling of Wall Street? It has been able to leverage its cash-rich balance sheet and aggressively pursue acquisitions, with a particular focus on companies that have developed technology solutions in energy storage. By acquiring innovative companies such as Ecobee, Pika, Enabla, and Neurio, Generac is now viewed by Wall Street as a technology play in the sustainable energy field instead of a traditional manufacturing company. The proof is in its price-to-earnings ratio. With over nine thousand global employees, Generac recently announced a $53-million planned investment in the state of Wisconsin. To kick off the commitment, it acquired a 75,000-square-foot office building in Pewaukee and stated a goal of hiring an additional seven hundred employees within the state. Generac's meteoric rise was not destiny. There were many bumps along the way, including the move to take the company public in 2010. Home standby generators are not unique, and Generac faced tough competitors right in its backyard from the likes of Briggs & Stratton and Kohler. Generac took a great product, put the right leadership in place, and out-executed the competition.

Important to note in the stories of Milwaukee Tool and Generac, both companies were able to attack additional business opportunities because they had sustainable cash flow from existing products that were already profitable, and they used it to fund growth. Every state is searching for the next breakthrough industry or product that will lead to an era of unrivaled prosperity. It's natural to want the next Apple to be developed right here in Madison or the next Microsoft to be founded in Appleton. But even if you are in an area like Silicon Valley, which possesses a deep bench of potential breakthrough companies, building an economic development strategy around startups is an incredibly risky proposition.

The Foxconn saga should serve as a reminder that a philosophy of public policy that "goes for broke" in creating a brand-new industry or cluster, without a prior track record of success in the market, is nothing more than a casino approach to growing your economy. As we continue to spend much time and effort relitigating the Foxconn incentive decisions and the perceived inadequacy of Wisconsin's tech startup ecosystem, many industrial companies in Wisconsin continue to quietly plug along and grow. They might not be the high-flying technology companies that are lavished with venture capital dollars, hire thousands of coders and sales professionals, and outfit opulent offices, but these companies are the bread and butter of Wisconsin's economic backbone. As we look for the companies that are going to carry us through the Decade of Industrial, think hand tools and home standby generators.

The problem is that many of these companies can't find the skilled workforce needed to expand in Wisconsin. For generations now, the path to success has been defined as pursuing a four-year degree, the only way to find the American Dream. So how do we move beyond that?

We need to change the narrative.

CHAPTER 3

FOUR YEARS OR BUST

WHEN SCOTT WALKER WAS ELECTED as Wisconsin's governor in 2010, the United States was just starting to pull out of the Great Recession. The pledge to create 250,000 jobs during his first term as governor was immediate bulletin board material for both supporters and opponents. Walker held up Tommy Thompson's tenure as the benchmark. One of Wisconsin's most successful and popular governors, Thompson took office in January of 1987 and oversaw the creation of 233,000 jobs during his first term.[6] Surely, with nearly one million more residents than Thompson had access to in 1986 and an economy back on its feet, Walker could hit 250,000. With Republican majorities in both the assembly and senate, Walker moved quickly to reduce taxes, remove regulations, and supercharge economic development. Finding another governor who matched Walker's enthusiasm in supporting manufacturing industries would have been difficult. But as the macroeconomy continued to rebound, the job numbers in Wisconsin didn't keep pace. As Walker prepared to run for a second term, it was evident he was not going to reach his goal—not even close. But why?

At its roots, growing an economy equates to population growth plus productivity growth. If you have a stagnant or declining population, *sustaining* an economy is very difficult, let alone growing one. A 3.6 percent cumulative population growth over the past decade places Wisconsin at thirty-fourth nationally.[7] While that growth rate is not spectacular, the state did add roughly twenty thousand people per year during this time frame. Population growth in Wisconsin has been frequently cited as a challenge that holds us back, and I do not disagree. I am not a demographer, economist, or statistician, but I do not believe the data tells the whole story. Wisconsin's industrial economy is no longer built for exponential job creation. Think of twentieth-century manufacturing powerhouses, such as Allis-Chalmers and Briggs & Stratton, that employed tens of thousands of people in the Milwaukee area at their peaks. The employment model of the past has forever changed. We produce more products with far fewer people. While this explanation helps, it doesn't go deep enough. After all, the population is still growing, and manufacturing is still expanding. A combination of these factors should support a workforce that is adding people. I believe a much bigger story line is in play. Who wants to work in an industrial job anymore?

THE UNIVERSITY CONUNDRUM

I was born in 1978, one of the last years of Gen X. The mass migration of high school students entering the four-year college path took off with my generation. My life story presents a microcosm of how we arrived at the industrial workforce cliff we are presently looking over. I did not come from a real estate family or a business family. We were the classic blue-collar family whose parents proudly worked themselves into the middle class. Both of my parents worked in manufacturing. My father eventually found his calling with a machinery sales and robotic integration company. My mother also held a handful of manufacturing positions as she balanced raising me and my two brothers. A four-year business degree was not a predetermined destiny for me. In fact, by November of my junior year in high school, going to college was improbable. My grades were floundering, and when I wasn't trying to earn money washing dishes at my part-time job, I was thinking ahead to my senior year of football.

I had enrolled in a masonry shop class at the start of my junior year. I found the idea of being outside doing physical labor rather intriguing. During shop class one morning, my teacher was discussing his plans for an upcoming deer hunt. The Wisconsin deer season was approaching, a near religious experience for blue-collar Wisconsinites. I began hunting with my dad when I turned twelve, and the week of gun season had quickly become one of my favorite weeks of the year. My teacher noted that masons would soon be shutting down for the winter. This was exciting to me. It seemed like masons led a pretty good life—make a bunch of money busting your butt through the grueling warm months and then have the winter off. Hunt, fish, snowmobile, maybe even go to Mexico for a couple of weeks. It seemed like a can't-miss proposition for a sixteen-year-old. I vividly remember going home and dropping the news to my parents at the dinner table. "You know

I've given this a lot of thought. I really like the idea of making twenty dollars an hour right out of school without taking on debt. I can even start next summer, before my senior year."

I expected my dad to be pleased. He had taken an interesting path to create the American Dream for our family, dropping out of high school at the age of sixteen and moving out of his parents' house to figure out life. I was expecting him to congratulate me on my independent decision, but he paused, processing what he wanted to say, and then made a request. "Tell you what, I know you have the capabilities to go on to a four-year school. All I am asking of you is to give it a try. You can always come back to being a mason. It's a noble profession. I have many friends who are masons. Yes, you are going to make great money when you are young. But my friends who are almost fifty years old have a hard time getting out of bed."

His comments hit me like a ton of bricks, and it was one of the rare occurrences that my sixteen-year-old self listened to my father. I refocused my academic efforts, signed up for the ACT, and began thinking about what business school I could get into. The masonry class was the first and last shop class that I took. My generation was the start of the parental shift in opinion that embraced pursuing a four-year degree over working in the traditional blue-collar industry.

I recall attending a manufacturing industry event in 2019 in which the keynote speaker asked more than three hundred attendees to raise their hands if they support the creation of manufacturing jobs in the United States. Ninety percent of the room raised their hands, and I suspect any holdouts were likely answering email on their phones. The speaker then followed up with his next question. "How many of you would be proud of your son or daughter if they came home and told you they were going to select a career in an entry-level manufacturing position?" I would be surprised if more than 40 percent of hands remained in the air.

Look back at the past three decades and consider the picture that society has painted for young adults looking to enter industrial careers. I think you can now answer why people aren't showing up. But how do we attempt to change public opinion? After all, we are swimming upstream against a current that has now been moving in the same direction for the better part of thirty years. Can we leverage the strengths of our past to solve our workforce challenges? Can industry lead the way?

CAN THE PAST LEAD OUR FUTURE?

Is the industrial economy of Wisconsin the horse and buggy trying to survive in the new world of the automobile? A remnant of a bygone era? Are we better off pursuing entrepreneurial startups in technology fields? Our economic future lies within our ability to answer these questions. Economic development policy tends to focus on what's next. Earlier in this book, I introduced the concept of the Decade of Industrial, an era in which I believe manufacturing and logistics will deliver substantial societal advancements and economic opportunities for Americans. But to be clear, many of the businesses that operate in industrial fields are not necessarily changing life as we know it; rather, they are incrementally improving our lives on a day-to-day basis. Think about a company that takes a forty-eight-hour delivery down to a same-day delivery. It is still delivering the same product; it is just delivering that product more quickly. These industrial companies are not the high-flying unicorns that can catapult toward massive valuations with bold projections of dominating new market verticals. Every state wants to target job creation in technology fields—software, apps, healthcare, bio med, and artificial intelligence. Yes, these fields will create many jobs of the future, but technology companies do not necessarily offer a panacea of economic growth. Only the *right* technology companies do. Many are intoxicated by the thought of creating billion-dollar market cap companies that change the way we live, but is it realistic to suggest that the state of Wisconsin can succeed in creating a Silicon Valley–like economy?

Epic Systems is one of Wisconsin's best-known technology companies and the type of startup a movie could be based on. Still a privately held company, Epic has scaled to over nine thousand employees and over $3 billion in annual revenue.[8] It occupies a vast, modern corporate campus in Verona that seems to expand with new futuristic buildings every year. New subdivisions and retail amenities pop up all over the Dane County area to support the company's continued growth. Epic's success is the definition of an economic development grand slam. It has been dominating the emerging field of electronic healthcare records management, but rarely do you hear the age of the company. Epic was founded in 1979, but most of its explosive growth occurred *after* being in business for thirty years. A world-changing technology is scalable only at the moment in time in which society is ready to embrace the change created. An economic development model that aggressively pursues technology businesses needs to be prepared for the volatility sure to follow. For this strategy to work, you either need: (a) a deep bench of candidates, or (b) luck...or (c) both! Take Foxconn as an example; they have hyped 5G, smart cities, and internet of things (IoT) as areas they plan to dominate, but to date, they have not made visible progress with a viable commercial product in any of these technologies.

To be clear, I am not an inflexible luddite who does not want to adapt to the future. I believe developing companies that are technology leaders within their industries is essential for the long-term viability of Wisconsin, but I also believe we must consider this: does Wisconsin have a better chance for long-term economic success by targeting its existing industrial businesses, or can we disrupt the established hierarchy of states who dominate the startup scene? Young entrepreneurs lament at the lack of fundraising alternatives available in Wisconsin, but I argue that the interest levels of the investment community reflect behaviors consistent with the culture of the state.

We are fiscally conservative people. We do not like striking out, even for the chance to land a big payday. Rather, we appreciate the grind of singles and doubles. State policies aimed at tax credits for high-net-worth individuals and more recent proposals to develop a "fund of funds" seeded by the general budget will not change our core behaviors. And while we can wait for the unicorns to arrive, our workhorses plod along with what they do best: make and provide things for everyday life. Many of these companies are already hubs of innovation, just not on a scale that changes life as we know it. The choice between new-age tech and old-line industrial does not have to be an "either/or" decision, but I believe we have a much better chance of success if we leverage our ingrained position of strength: our existing industrial base.

Much of the conversation around recruiting people to the state has been targeted at future, college-educated young professionals. Think back to the WEDC campaign from 2016 to 2018, which was focused on the Chicago market. You cannot fault the attempt, but are young professionals working in large, urban cities the best candidates to convince to move to Wisconsin? As an HR director of a prominent Wisconsin manufacturer (whose name shall remain anonymous) told me, "It's great that we want people with four-year degrees in this state. We're all for it. But I can tell you we are appropriately staffed in our four-year degree positions. What I need right now is one hundred employees who can just show up in our plant, work hard, and we'll train them with the technical skills that they need to grow."

Thoughtful conversations on what economic sectors the state needs to pursue are healthy and necessary. Certainly perspectives contrary to my belief that the old-line industry can provide the pathway to future prosperity are worth considering. Any route must still solve for the biggest challenge facing employers in the state of Wisconsin: finding enough people to staff available jobs.

CHAPTER 4

THE GEARS ARE GRINDING

> "The definition of insanity is doing the same thing
> over and over again and expecting different results."
> —ALBERT EINSTEIN

THE DEMOGRAPHIC CLIFF FACING industrial employers did not suddenly show up postpandemic. What began as a tiny snowflake around 2010 became a snowball as it started to slowly tumble down the hill, accelerating and gradually growing into a larger and larger mass through the decade, until finally the pandemic delivered an avalanche warning at the bottom of the mountain.

Suzanne Kelley, President and CEO of the Waukesha County Business Alliance (WCBA) since 2009, has been sitting front row listening to the workforce plight over the past decade. Prior to her current role, she spent twenty-three years as the Midwest Government Relations Lead for General Electric. Suzanne is someone you turn to in southeast Wisconsin if you want to get something done. She combines a unique skillset of deep philosophical understanding with a disposition for action. Serving as CEO of the chamber for one of the state's economic hubs provides a unique perspective as to what is driving business, both good and bad.

Suzanne recalls that when she started in 2009, industrial employers were just starting to peer over the horizon and understand workforce challenges lay ahead. The early 2000s was an era in which US manufacturing accelerated global expansion and outsourcing alternatives over domestic investments. The decade concluded with the crippling Great Recession. As the economy started to recover in early 2011, manufacturers began reaching out to Suzanne and her team to start a conversation about the negative perceptions and biases showing up in public discourse regarding careers in manufacturing. The industry was viewed as dark, dirty, and dangerous. The existing workforce was predominantly a baby boomer demographic who was going to start retiring en masse beginning around 2020. More importantly, there wasn't a farm system to attract new talent into industrial labor. The K–12 education system had abandoned any pretense of supporting industrial careers. Nearly all career planning guidance offered to students was of the "four-year college or bust" mentality.

The noise got louder as the economy started coming back to life. Manufacturing companies wanted to know what needed to happen to change the narrative. Suzanne saw this predicted problem slowly coming to life several years ago. "We were already hearing in the 2011 time frame that many of our industrial employers were alarmed with the ten-year labor outlook. What's rather interesting, and disappointing, is that this challenge is not a surprise. I think the bigger surprise is that the demographics look even more dire over the coming ten years."

The WCBA took note of the ever-expanding list of companies calling its office looking for help. Many were manufacturing companies that traditionally would not have joined a chamber of commerce with a membership base heavy on service providers. Suzanne and her team capitalized on a need by forming the Manufacturing Executive Council. The Executive Council is a subgroup within the alliance, created specifically to meet the needs of its manufacturers. Priority number one was workforce development.

ROME WASN'T BUILT IN A DAY

Many business leaders believe that quick-fix solutions need to be delivered to instantaneously ease labor market strains. That path is no longer an option. A problem of this magnitude cannot be solved with overnight solutions. Doing so would be like steering a new course with a tanker ship—you just can't turn on a dime. The manufacturing industry got a bad rap, some would say self-imposed, from many actions taken over time. This has led to an era in which we are now spanning three generations (Gen X, millennials, and Gen Z) who have shunned career opportunities in industrial fields. A mindset shift is needed. For private enterprises that need people to survive, a key strategic role of the business must be involved in recruiting. Finding industrial workers is almost like running a collegiate athletic program. Companies are responsible for defining who their ideal candidates are and developing a game plan to recruit them from the high school system. Companies need to be out in the community telling their stories.

Suzanne references Waukesha-based Superior Crane as a success story that emerged from the Manufacturing Executive Council program. Superior Crane certainly fits the profile of your classic privately held Wisconsin manufacturing business. From a plant on the southside of Waukesha, it builds and services lifting systems, such as large overhead bridge cranes needed to move heavy material. Frustrated with the available labor pool (or lack thereof), it went on the offensive and developed a program called Superior Crane University that aims to attract high-school-age students to a career in manufacturing. Superior Crane views the program as an opportunity to develop a future pipeline of talent. Students are not only immersed in the skillsets needed to be successful in manufacturing but they also are exposed to the abundant amount of career opportunities available in industrial occupations and are learning the Superior Crane business. This is an example of how industrial employers start to turn the tide. You need K–12 students engaged in understanding what career paths look like. WCBA also has had tremendous success with its Schools to Skills™ program that covers thirteen school districts across the county of Waukesha. The program connects manufacturers with local schools and arranges guided facility tours. Suzanne has been amazed by the willingness of her manufacturing members to share best practices. She explains:

With the labor market as tight as it has been, and no end in sight, it is a pleasant surprise that our Manufacturing Alliance members are an open book to each other in sharing best practices. There is a general mindset that if the [manufacturing community] cannot band together to elevate the profile of the available careers, the task of making the field more attractive will just not get done.

As Suzanne looks over the horizon of the 2020s, she sees much opportunity within the challenges that lie ahead for industrial companies.

Available labor is hands down the number-one challenge our members face. In fact, when I joined the Alliance, many business leaders viewed excessive taxes and regulations as the state's top challenge. Today, those issues are often viewed through a workforce lens—how can we get Wisconsin out of the top ten in terms of tax burden so we can attract more people to our state? We need to be all in on solving this problem from many angles. I see it as a triangle approach of (1) private industry, (2) education, and (3) government. As we sit here today, all three must work together on better alignment with what needs to get done.

Suzanne believes that industry has led the conversation and education is starting to come around, but government has been the laggard in progressively advancing an actionable agenda that produces results. What would Suzanne do if she were governor for a day and could issue two executive actions that would make an impact?

We need to completely reconstruct and realign the state's efforts around workforce development. This area is changing so rapidly, and we just are not keeping up. There needs to be a task force of private industry, education, and government that creates an actionable plan that carries achievable benchmarks. Define how many people we are going to need and how we are going to get them. The second thing we need to do is create more incentive and education programs for small- to medium-sized industrial companies to lead them through the technology and automation transformation that is occurring throughout industry.

Suzanne is a big believer that change starts at the local level. Each region of the state has different needs and different cultural norms. A one-size-fits-all approach is not the solution here. We need all our industry leaders to get in the game, we need our education system to embrace the available career opportunities, and we need the government to align around achievable goals and to make smart investments that support those goals. But in the end, it all comes down to the people. Underdogs are underdogs for a reason, but they overcome the odds all the time. They just need contributions from the entire team and magic can happen.

THE FARM SYSTEM

Eighty-five postsecondary campuses are sprinkled throughout the state of Wisconsin. We possess a deep and accessible education system, which represents a distinct competitive advantage to the residents and businesses of this state. As I covered previously, industry has been agonizing over the worker skills gap for the better part of the past decade.

We know that jobs available in today's industry demand a much more advanced skillset than they used to, and we also know that job opportunities continue to go unfilled. Is this strictly a numbers game, or are we missing a bigger picture? The propensity for society to funnel kids into the four-year-college model undoubtedly siphoned away willing and able students who otherwise would have been attracted to a technical degree. To be clear, a robust four-year system is essential for the long-term viability of the state; we need the very best and brightest minds to innovate and create. But I also believe that if you asked your average Wisconsin industrial business whether they need a four-year marketing major or an employee who can manage a team of robots, the majority would take the robot manager right now. If our goal is to grow the worker pool attracted to industrial jobs, we need a laser-like focus on the outcomes being produced through the state's technical colleges and the vocational school system. Roughly 250,000 people per year enroll into Wisconsin's technical college system, and we know we are producing results. A whopping 91 percent of our technical college graduates are employed within six months of graduating, and 94 percent are staying right here in Wisconsin to live and work.[9] We are producing skilled job candidates—just not enough of them. Like several of Wisconsin's economic challenges, much of the problem comes from our inability to articulate the value proposition. There is a story to tell the next generation about our technical college system, and I am going to start with one right in my backyard, Waukesha County Technical College (WCTC).

Rich Barnhouse began his role as president of WCTC in January of 2021. I was able to sit down with him and discuss some of his perspectives on the challenges and opportunities we must address as we attempt to take on the ongoing skills and labor gap challenges. But before we get into that, it is important to understand a little bit more about his background.

Rich cut a unique path through life leading up to becoming president of one of the top technical college programs in the state. He grew up outside of Toronto, Canada, and was raised in a meat processing and packing family business—about as blue collar as it gets. While he certainly didn't appreciate the lessons he was learning at the time, the experience had a profound impact on his life. Rich shared a personal story that led him out of the family business and into the world of higher education. In his teenage years, he and his younger brother were tasked with cleaning out a meat gutter at the end of a long shift. Nothing about meatpacking would qualify as glamorous; however, cleaning the meat gutter was about as nauseating as it got. Rich recalls that they were both laughing hysterically as they attacked the job in disgust. Upon completion of removing all the meat scraps, his brother made the proclamation that he was done with the family business and going to college for a degree that could land him a job in anything but meat packing. Rich followed suit and went on to receive a four-year degree in exercise psychology from Brock University, a master's degree in sports administration from Central Michigan, and a PhD from Cardinal Stritch University.

Rich had a vision for his life, and the industrial world was certainly not part of it. Rich's career epiphany came while he was employed at Rice University. An elite institution, Rice attracts students who have the ambition, drive, and talent to do big things in their lives. They are among the best of the best. Oftentimes, in awe of the sheer genius of the students he was working with, Rich realized that those kids were going to make it with or without a great teacher by their side. Rich yearned to make an impact with students who needed more direction and didn't have the network or resources to get them through. He presented to me a deep, personal belief that succinctly articulates his mission: "There is a genius on every corner; we just need to get their brains and skills to the table." Upon discovering his new mission, Rich felt his childhood roots in manufacturing pulling him back toward the technical college system, which ultimately led him to Wisconsin. After stints as the associate vice chancellor for the UW two-year campuses, dean of students at Moraine Park Technical College, and vice president at the State College of Florida, he landed his present role as president of WCTC.

Rich brings an outsider's perspective and pulls from unique life experiences when looking to solve the labor crunch challenges. Being a Gen Xer, he often finds himself playing the role of Switzerland when it comes to connecting the dots between baby boomer business owners and the millennial and Gen Z workforce they are trying to attract. He is standing at the front lines of the battle to bring more people into industrial and Industry 4.0 careers, and he has a rather large audience to produce results for. WCTC is located in the middle of Waukesha County, a primary economic hub for the state of Wisconsin with a huge industrial base. Thousands of businesses are based there, including manufacturing heavyweights such as Harley-Davidson, Eaton, GE Healthcare, and Quad.

Waukesha County, much like the state of Wisconsin, has a math problem on its hands. WCTC commissioned a study that points to a 12.4 percent cumulative decline of Waukesha County High School seniors from 2022 to 2032.[10] A declining birth rate is accelerating across the state. Live births in Wisconsin fell to 60,615 in 2020, a roughly 16 percent drop from 2007, which was the year prior to the Great Recession setting in.[11] We are literally just hitting the tip of the workforce iceberg. While the near-term demographic trends are going to continue to present problems for companies throughout Wisconsin, the state is certainly not unique in facing this challenge. This is a national problem, which means we can still compete and win if we can figure out how to do more with less. While being a realist, Rich also is quite optimistic that the state can continue to provide the necessary growth environment needed for its industrial companies. We discussed three trends that have emerged from the pandemic that will radically impact the workforce conversation over the years to come:

1. Wage appreciation for industrial jobs has changed the conversation. Money influences career choice, and WCTC can point to examples in which its students are making $50,000 to $80,000 a year within a couple of years of graduating.[12]

2. Companies are rapidly turning to automation to solve their labor problems. Rich estimates that the lack of available labor has pulled forward automation strategies three to five years.

3. The state needs to decrease the time to complete a college degree by offering high school juniors and seniors the opportunity to enroll full-time in college while still in high school, thereby earning their high school diplomas and college associate degrees simultaneously.

I will cover the movement to automation in the next chapter, but a critical theme that continues to tie the technical college system and the industrial job market together is education and training. The days of dropping out of high school and showing up at the local plant for a lifetime of employment are long gone. With the ongoing evolution of technology, careers in many industrial fields require a strong background in math, science, and computer programming. On the surface, this might appear to be another challenge for industrial companies, but it also presents an opportunity to attract more talented people away from competing fields. Rich noted that WCTC's auto mechanic lab now primarily trains future mechanics through computer systems, not with greasy wrenches. WCTC is focusing its education offerings on the future and not the past. It will soon have a complete battery cell lab designed to train auto techs for the coming electrification of the auto fleet. What is happening at WCTC certainly does not reflect the industrial career vision imparted upon me as a teenager.

Rich's diverse background and travels across the United States have brought an outsider's perspective to the local technical college system. He is not tied to the "this is how we have always done it" orthodoxy. An open and determined mind is going to be required of any leader looking to make an impact in workforce development over the coming decade. Industry

4.0 is here, and while much of the data supports the continued decline of workforce participants, Rich believes that Wisconsin is in good shape to be recognized as a leader in workforce training and preparation. Why is this?

WISCONSIN'S UNIQUE ADVANTAGE: A STRONG PUBLIC-PRIVATE RELATIONSHIP

Rich commented that the relationship between the private sector and the technical college system in Wisconsin is about as strong as he has observed throughout the country. Ongoing day-to-day collaboration is occurring between the parties, which promotes a continuous evolution of in-demand curriculum. Rich believes that this is a unique advantage for Wisconsin and a dynamic that many other states cannot boast of. The governance structure of the Wisconsin technical college system is also rather advantageous in maneuvering through the challenges of the current time frame. It starts with accountability. As president of WCTC, Rich reports to a board of local taxpayers throughout the county of Waukesha. The current board is made up of private-sector business executives, a trade union executive, and a school superintendent. These people are living the day-to-day challenges of industry, and they all have a vested interest in producing results. Rich gets to hear feedback in real time. Employers can let him know what they expect of his students, and the college can pivot quickly to tweak or create a curriculum that aligns with the new standards of industry.

Another key advantage of the Wisconsin technical college system is its reliance on advisory committees, committees made up of local industry professionals who advise colleges regarding the curriculum for programs. This concept seems anathema to how the traditional four-year model is operated. Wisconsin companies have excellent access to the technical college system, and perhaps the greatest strength our state possesses is the willingness of many employers to roll up their sleeves and get involved with the local tech college on the proper training for the equipment and processes students need to succeed when they graduate.

Back to being a realist, numbers are numbers. We still need to find the people who want to take jobs in industrial fields. Rich and I further discussed the perception of industrial careers, manufacturing in particular. Over much of the past three decades, the K–12 education system has been delivering a message to its students that championed the necessity of a four-year degree. This message has come from guidance counselors, teachers, and, most importantly, parents. Rich started to observe a shift in how the K–12 system viewed industrial careers around 2015. Local school boards began receiving an earful of discontent from the industrial companies. Young industrial labor was nowhere to be found, and no one was telling students about the new career opportunities available in modern facilities with family-supporting wages and benefits. But, slowly but surely, the image of working for an industrial company is changing, at least in Wisconsin.

WCTC recently hosted a tour for approximately fifty Hartland Arrowhead high school students. Those numbers were unthinkable five years ago. The interest is starting to come back, and the narrative is changing. Kids can make middle-class wages by the time they are twenty years old while participating in industrial careers much more technical and fulfilling than the assembly lines of the past. All the while, they are avoiding racking up the exorbitant student debt that often comes with a four-year degree. While we are making progress with many K–12 school systems, the bigger challenge might lie within the wishes of students' parents. Many parents are still not coming around to the opportunities available for their children in industrial occupations. Rich has two ideas on how we can change perceptions:

> Industrial operations and WCTC need to do a much better job of marketing themselves to the public. There are two areas that the message needs to focus on. Number one: we (manufacturing companies) are hiring you (job candidates) to lead with your brains and your problem-solving skills, and sometimes you will use your physical skills. Number two: employers and WCTC need to start openly promoting the financial benefits of an industrial career. I am finding that the next wave of talent, Gen Z, is very driven to succeed, and economics matter to them. You need to talk about what kind of pay they can expect and, perhaps most importantly, what their future earning potential is.

During my conversation with Rich, our attention turned to what Wisconsin's technical colleges and vocational education system will look like in 2030. What would Rich do if he were governor for a day and could issue two executive actions to make an impact? His first action would be passing legislation that blends different education platforms into a fully comprehensive system from kindergarten through postgraduate degree. We need to do a better job of customizing curriculum for students at a much younger age. This will better prepare them for career paths that align with their talents and skillsets. As an example, my children's school district, Kettle Moraine (KM), has produced excellent results from creating specialized charter-school programs and off-campus partnerships through the high school. Some of the alternatives include the Advanced Manufacturing Certificate Program, High School of Health and Sciences, and KM Global. Kids are able to get their general high school education *and* get hands-on experience in careers they might have interest in.

A second action that Rich would pursue is further increasing student accessibility through increasing transportation alternatives. One of every four students at WCTC lives in Milwaukee County, and getting to class can be an issue. Rich suggested that a dedicated high-speed rail line initially focused on key stops throughout the Milwaukee-to-Madison corridor would be a huge differentiator for the region and his preferred method to solve the issue. While a rail line might not be achievable over the coming decade, providing enhanced bussing service for students would be incredibly beneficial for many of the students of WCTC.

The education system must become more effective and efficient in moving students through the system in a timely fashion. The ability for Wisconsin to navigate a couple of minor changes in how we integrate the different education models will be a huge determinant in how we successfully prepare students for future careers. Both society as a whole and the individual suffer if we continue perpetuating a system that encourages prolonging the education process. Increasing the portability of credits is low-hanging fruit for the state. If a class is passed at an accredited Wisconsin institution, the credit should be easily transferred to an alternate school. As it stands today, Wisconsin is ranked second to last in the country for a student's ability to transfer credits from a two-year school to a four-year school.[13] This is primarily the result of a law designed to restrict the portability of earned credits, passed in 1973. This places an unnecessary burden on the mobility of a student to move through the education system, which leads to more time in college, more student debt, and less available workforce. If a student passes a class at an accredited state institution and the credits are applicable to the education path the student is pursuing, the credits should count within the state system.

Rich concluded our conversation with his vision of the path that lies ahead:

Artificial intelligence, machine learning, robotics, battery technology—the state of Wisconsin has everything in place to be a leader in all of these fields. Industry 4.0 has arrived, and we have the companies, we have the people, and we have the education system. What we will need more than anything is a mindset that will allow for us to adapt at a pace that most of our traditional institutions, both public and private, will not be comfortable with. Adapting will not be easy, but it's also not a choice.

While both Rich and I believe that more and more people from the Gen Z and iGen cohorts will continue to be drawn into industrial fields, we still face an immediate future in which retirements will likely outpace new entrants to industrial careers. To get through to the other side, man is going to need machine.

CHAPTER 5

AUTOMATE OR DIE

"For most purposes, a man with a machine is
better than a man without a machine."
—HENRY FORD

THE GREAT RECESSION TIME FRAME of 2008 to 2010 was a
jolting blow to the psyche of the country. The real-estate-fueled
exuberance of the 2000s concluded with a hard, abrupt stop.
An estimated 3.8 million Americans suffered a foreclosure,[14]
legacy US financial behemoths such as Bear Stearns were literally wiped out overnight, and 8.6 million jobs were lost.[15]

While the shock to the system impacted all Americans
for roughly three years, the communities and families that
depended on manufacturing jobs had already developed a
thick callus, formed over the preceding decade leading up to
the Great Recession. Starting around the year 2000, US manufacturing companies either embraced or succumbed to globalization and hemorrhaged manufacturing jobs; 5.7 million jobs,
or 33 percent of the total US manufacturing workforce, were
cut from 2000 to 2010.[16] As we emerged from the ashes of the
Great Recession, the prospects of a new age of manufacturing
looked rather bleak.

AUTOMATION: A SURPRISING JOB CREATOR?

The 2010s didn't quite play out as many had predicted. A gradual transition to the automation of plants and processes was supposed to continue the downward slide of overall industry employment. The opposite has been true. Surprisingly, 1.4 million manufacturing jobs were added to the US economy in the 2010s, and we hear each and every day that employers need more and more people just to keep up.[17] What did the prognosticators miss? Effective investment in technology usually creates more business opportunities for companies, which expands their reach and markets, which necessitates more job creation...that is, *if* employers can find qualified applicants.

The inevitable wave of baby boomer retirements has accelerated as we emerge from the pandemic. Supply and demand forces continue to push up wages, which are needed to attract an ever-shrinking labor pool. Industrial companies are now advertising on billboards, hyping starting pay increases to over $18 per hour plus the allure of thousands of dollars in signing bonuses. Think about the reaction you would have received from your friends if you would have made that prediction back in 2010!

Finding manual labor, once taken for granted as an unlimited resource, is a challenge for everyone. To compete, technology becomes a strategic pillar for all industrial businesses. And with advanced technologies comes a need for a better-trained and nimbler workforce. Success in Industry 4.0 for the United States will demand the integration of man and machine. "Onshoring" or "nearshoring" opportunities are generating much excitement, but manual manufacturing of low-margin and high-volume products will still be rather difficult in the US, if not impossible. Think back to the original iteration of the one-million-square-foot Foxconn LCD facility. When the plan was initially announced, industry experts across the globe were shocked by the suggestion that a competitively priced LCD screen could be produced in the United States, even with the heavy incentives that were offered. The future of US manufacturing will continue to be in creating and adding value domestically and pushing mass production elsewhere. Substantial growth opportunities lay ahead for the companies and communities that can attract both the human capital *and* technology capital required to win.

THE BOOMER GENERATION: NO SHORTAGE OF PEOPLE

Without getting too deep into a history lesson, I want to acknowledge a critical component that drove US manufacturing through the twentieth century: access to people. Up until recent times, manufacturing in the United States has had little problem accessing labor. More importantly, how the United States was positioned immediately after World War II set the stage for global economic dominance. The United States tragically lost 416,800 lives in World War II, but our casualties paled in comparison to the rest of the world, both in human life and property. Outside of Pearl Harbor, the war did not touch US soil. With the end of the war in 1945, the United States was the lone superpower left standing that had both the people and the factories needed to supply a world that had been destroyed.

GIs returned home to jobs waiting for them in factories that were going to produce the products needed to rebuild countries around the globe. The returning GIs also got busy creating families. The baby boomer generation was about to sprout, and there was going to be more than enough people for decades to come.

We have addressed the current challenges that many employers have in not only growing but also simply sustaining a workforce. It is about to get much more difficult. The guarantee of a limitless supply of labor has passed the United States by. Birth rates in the United States have been on a decade-long slide. The average lifetime replacement rate per female hit an alarming 1.64 births per woman in 2020. We need 2.1 just to stay above water.[18] Further complicating the employment picture, manufacturing careers have been eschewed for alternative career paths. Fewer overall people in the world, plus fewer people interested in working in the field, is a tough math problem.

Demographic trends over the next decade do not look any more promising. Even with our best efforts to pull more people into industrial fields, the cold hard facts do not support a scenario in which manufacturers will be able to fulfill growth opportunities through the addition of manual labor alone. The transition to automation of industrial processes is the only way out. The United States is not exactly a pioneer in this experiment. Out of necessity, global manufacturing giants such as Japan and Germany pursued a manufacturing policy of automation soon after World War II because they simply did not have enough people.

CROSSING THE THRESHOLD

Kent Lorenz is one of the sharpest minds in manufacturing that I have had the pleasure to meet. He was born and raised in Wisconsin and graduated from UW-Madison in 1984 with a degree in engineering physics. His career path placed him in leadership roles at several market-leading machine tool sales and robotics integration companies, including Ellison Machinery (now known as Ellison Technologies) and Acieta. In 2018 UW-Madison recognized his impactful career in manufacturing with its Distinguished Achievement Award for his work in industrial robotics. Kent possesses the rare blend of technical brilliance required of an engineer and emotional and people intelligence necessary for sales and leadership.

Kent is now "retired" but still serves on five public and private company boards, including four manufacturers. Kent and his wife, Abby, continue to reside in Wisconsin year-round. Retirement for Kent is not playing golf in the sun. He wants to be in the mix, and he wants to help the state's industrial economy any way he can. Speaking to Kent about manufacturing gives you the feeling of watching Aaron Rodgers sizing up the opposing defense right before he takes the snap. He is completely in the zone—past, present, and, more importantly, future. Kent is exactly the type of person who needs to be at the table as we discuss how to develop solutions for our industrial companies as they look to dominate the Decade of Industrial.

Kent began his manufacturing journey in 1984, and his career spanned a time frame of complete transformation of Wisconsin manufacturing. The recession of the early 1980s hit legacy Wisconsin manufacturers like Allis-Chalmers and A. O.

Smith incredibly hard. Milwaukee County shed over 30 percent of its manufacturing workforce from 1979 - 1984. 50,000 jobs gone in just under five years.[19] Prior to 1980, Milwaukee had been a thriving economy that built things; it had a robust middle class that exploded when the GIs returned from World War II. The 1980s delivered a drastic change. The Machine Shop of the World was suddenly the home of old and shuttered industry. The Rust Belt was born, and Milwaukee was part of the family.

Recall the demographic trends I cited in the previous section. The concept of a labor shortage is a recent phenomenon in the United States, but as baby boomers transition into retirement, we need to be prepared for the avalanche of departures on the horizon. Kent cited a couple of eye-opening comments from a recent Wisconsin Workforce report:

Wisconsin is projected to need twenty-five thousand new people per year in manufacturing just to keep up with growth. But there are upwards of seventy-five thousand baby boomers who will be retiring every year for the foreseeable future, so we now need one hundred thousand workers per year just to keep up. As a businessperson, you must come to terms with the reality that your dependence on manual labor has fundamentally changed. You need to design your operations around your technology and fill in the people around it, which is going to be very difficult for many companies who have operated with the next-person-up approach since the end of World War II.

This mindset shift will not come easily for policy makers. Creating new jobs, the gold standard of economic development prowess, can no longer be how we define success. It is time for the state to fundamentally change the way it views economic development. The incentive conversation has traditionally started and ended with how many jobs are either being created or saved. We must confront the fact that demographic challenges, along with changing career preferences, will continue to limit job growth opportunities within traditional industrial fields. While trying to change the career narrative, slogans like, "This isn't your father's manufacturing!" and "Manufacturing is no longer dumb, dirty, and dangerous!" aren't exactly a call to action to drop what you are doing and pursue a career path in manufacturing. When analyzing economies like Wisconsin that depend on manufacturing, capital investment and growing output need to be the key metrics. Technology costs money, usually a lot of it, and investment in technology is certainly not a risk-free proposition. We need our industrial companies focused on capital investment and expenditure, but that's not what gets a community excited. The big job announcement is what gets people elected and keeps them in office. To remain globally competitive, Wisconsin needs to incentivize its companies to invest in automation and technology.

While we have entered a rather turbulent time frame for manufacturing, Kent is a big believer that Wisconsin's best days lie ahead:

I believe that manufacturing in 2030, only eight years away, will produce 30 percent more but will have 30 percent fewer companies. If you can position yourself on the cutting edge of automation and innovation, there will be nearly limitless opportunities to grow your business. You will not have a choice either. If you cannot commit to the type of investment needed to sustain a technological edge, you will not survive.

The rate of industry change is accelerating at a breakneck pace, even for well-capitalized global giants. Wisconsin's industrial economy is made up of many small- to medium-sized privately held businesses that are not necessarily geared up with the resources needed to navigate the rapid transition. Kent brought up his thirty-plus years of experience in selling technologically advanced systems to Wisconsin manufacturers:

It was difficult in 1984 and it has not changed much since; we always had much greater success in selling cutting-edge technology to companies throughout the United States before the companies in Wisconsin adapted. The conservative nature in Wisconsin just takes more time to review investment alternatives and commit. Technology is changing so fast that many of the smaller employers just are not set up to keep up with the technology they invested in last year, yet alone what is coming online next year.

With our manufacturing heritage and blue-chip roster of manufacturing companies already located here, Wisconsin has a massive opportunity to attract new capital investment in automation, robotics, and technology on the shop floors throughout the state. Naysayers will suggest that automation will eliminate jobs. I do not agree with this premise. Much more productivity and value is generated from companies that continue to capture market share with increased productivity and better service offerings, which is then leveraged into a higher-yielding workforce and additional investments. Creative destruction succeeds in replacing antiquated industry processes with a new path to prosperity. This concept has propelled the United States to command the most powerful global economy in two short centuries. But even if you take the position that automation is, at best, a zero-sum game for employment, meaning investing in technology might lead to a decline in manufacturing positions, my response is: What's the alternative? Where are we going to find the people? We are now at a point where investing in automation and technology is required for basic survival.

Kent has observed the technology plight of small- to medium-sized enterprises for three decades. A significant challenge with the adoption of technology for many companies is financing. Technology is incredibly capital intensive. For some businesses, just three to four robotic cells can exceed the value of their buildings. Due to collateral risk, traditional lenders such as banks are reluctant to lend on technology investment. If anything goes south on the loan, antiquated technology does not hold residual value, and, in some cases, you might not even be able to give it away. Banks want to lend when they know they can get paid back with, for example, traditional collateral or a building. Real estate presents an asset that the bank knows will hold intrinsic value. If the bank must call the loan, it knows it can monetize the asset and salvage some of the outstanding debt. Without traditional lenders participating in the financing of technology, a key source of firepower sits on the sidelines. This dynamic creates an environment in which businesses need to use their free cash to upgrade their automation and technology stack—not the most efficient way to scale growth opportunities. Additionally, the lack of financing alternatives has an outsized impact on smaller businesses who might not yet have the free cash flow to support self-funded investment.

What would Kent do if he were governor for a day and could issue two executive actions that would help move manufacturing forward? First and foremost, he would create a dedicated lending program for the state of Wisconsin specifically tailored toward investment in automation and technology. Possible outcomes could be establishing two different types of lending programs, the first catered toward small businesses that are taking the leap into investment and the second designed for medium-sized businesses looking to scale their existing technology into market-leading positions. The Paycheck Protection Plan (PPP) model that was rolled out during the pandemic could create a framework for a targeted lending program designed to facilitate financing for small businesses. A public–private relationship could be created to oversee the lending facility, and loans made through private-sector lenders could carry an interest expense and could be backstopped by the state. Loan forgiveness schedules could also be considered based upon performance metrics. In a biennium budget approaching $90 billion and an economy that continues to produce a significant tax surplus, seeding $100 million in the next budget cycle is a reasonable target for a lending fund specific to investment in automation and technology that will assist in growing industrial operations throughout the state of Wisconsin.

ANOTHER WISCONSIN ADVANTAGE

Kent's second action if he were governor for a day is specific to the macro field of emerging technology in manufacturing. He believes Wisconsin posseses a hidden gem of innovation in the Wisconsin Alumni Research Foundation (WARF), which is underfunded given the results being produced. The state could supercharge economic development by doubling down on WARF's total annual budget. WARF's total budget in 2021 was just over $100 million, of which $22 million is allocated toward additional support for the development, patenting, licensing, and commercializing of emerging technologies being developed through the program. WARF has helped facilitate the development of over two thousand patents and 645 commercial licensees. The best part? The patents are for tangible products and processes meant to improve people's lives. WARF's technology portfolio covers a wide range of categories, including analytical instrumentation, pharmaceuticals, food products, agriculture, research tools, medical devices, pluripotent stem cells, clean technology, information technology, and semiconductors.[20] Kent is personally involved in C-Motive Technologies, a WARF innovation founded by three UW PhDs. C-Motive has developed an electrostatic motor that is one-third the weight and ten times the torque of the existing competitive product in the market. Its mission is to create electric machines that directly reduce carbon emissions through empowering higher-efficiency renewable generators, enabling the next generation of e-mobility, and delivering more efficient industrial torque motors.[21] Kent is an investor in the enterprise and also serves on its board.

Discussing WARF led Kent and I back to a frequent challenge the Wisconsin entrepreneurial ecosystem struggles with; we are woefully behind in funding alternatives for early-stage businesses. Kent believes the state has one of the best idea-incubator systems in the United States, but we are not producing results in commercialization. He notes, "If the state wants to move the needle on economic development, we need to Ten X the commitment to WARF. The innovations coming out of WARF align with what we do in this state. We *make things*."

I like the idea of Ten X to help us make things in Wisconsin. Taking the $22 million that currently funds the commercialization initiatives at WARF to $200 million is a goal we need to achieve. We can create explosive growth opportunities for businesses we already have right in our backyard. Give them the tools they need to grow at home, and we will keep more of our UW grads right here in Wisconsin. But that begs the question, "Where are all the people going to live?"

CHAPTER 6

BUILDING THE RIGHT ANSWER

> "If you define the problem correctly, you almost have the solution."
> —STEVE JOBS

YOU HAVE LIKELY MET A NEW neighbor or business colleague who relocated to Wisconsin for a job opportunity. Many people who are transplants to the state have never visited here before, and it is not uncommon for them to arrive projecting a sense of apathy. They want to serve their time and get out as soon as possible. While I am sure we will never be able to convert some people to Wisconsinites, my personal experience with one of these new neighbors suggests that we have a pretty good track record of changing minds. Given a little time to adapt to our lifestyle, they quickly embrace the opportunity to build new lives for their families and never want to leave.

Quality of life and affordability are frequently championed as key attributes of enjoying life in Wisconsin. People relocated from the coasts often marvel at the perceived low cost of the housing stock available in our market. The cost of housing is an ever-escalating challenge across the United States, and

Wisconsin has not been immune. A home is often the single largest asset a family owns, and the run-up in housing values has provided a big boost to the net worth of existing homeowners. But limited inventory combined with rapidly escalating prices presents a big downside if you are a community looking to grow your working-age population. If Wisconsin's industrial companies want to attract a workforce that aligns with current compensation offerings, abundant housing alternatives become a key plank of economic development policy. Affordable workforce housing is an opportunity to build a unique advantage for the state of Wisconsin. We already possess a few key ingredients needed for success: plenty of land with limited geographic constraints and access to fresh water.

Creating more housing alternatives is also an objective goal that can be measured. I believe that Wisconsin can be recognized as a national leader in providing abundant workforce housing options by the end of this decade. How does this sound for the goal?

> Wisconsin will position itself as a national leader in providing affordable workforce housing solutions for its middle class. We will define success by annually delivering fifteen thousand new owner-occupied, single-family homes across the state through 2030. The additional units will ease the current inventory crunch and return real estate appreciation to its historical normal range. Succeeding at this goal will provide many more alternatives for residents of Wisconsin, allowing them to spend no more than 30 percent of their annual gross income on housing.

This is a SMART goal: specific, measurable, achievable, relevant, and time-bound. Most importantly, it is a goal that most people can agree with. Sure, there will be disagreements on *how* we get there, but the *why* is one of those rare opportunities that can coalesce both ends of the political spectrum, meaning we can get policy changes accomplished. Having a growing population of middle-income families is critically important if we want to be serious about addressing labor shortages over the coming decade. Multifamily development will play a role in providing additional housing options, but I believe single-family home ownership proves to be a more effective amenity in building a proud community with committed residents. The state of Wisconsin must become a leader in creating an environment in which its industrial workforce can obtain affordable *single-family* residences. Now for the hard part. How do we deliver workforce housing in the current environment?

THE REALITY OF HOME PRICES

If you have recently been in the market to buy a home, you know firsthand the difficulties of navigating the current environment. Inventory is limited and prices seem to increase daily, especially for homes priced under $350,000. The combination of record demand and limited supply has profoundly impacted affordability across the state. Existing home values have appreciated roughly 25 percent since late fall 2019,[22] and the Wisconsin Realtors Association noted in September of 2021 that median pricing across the state had already increased 9.6 percent in just the first nine months of the year. Despite the rapid run-up of pricing, insatiable consumer demand dwindled available inventory to only three months of supply by that fall.[23] While the pandemic acted as an accelerant for the housing shortage and brought the problem to a head, the supply and demand imbalance throughout the state of Wisconsin had been building since the real estate crash of the Great Recession. Building permits in southeast Wisconsin topped out in 2005 at roughly 17,500 and hasn't cracked more than 10,000 for over a decade.[24]

Wisconsin Housing Starts 2006-2019

Wisconsin Builders Association https://www.wisbuild.org/housing-data

This controlled development helped the market work through the hangover of the Great Recession but has also led to an environment in which demand is far outpacing supply. The price of an existing single-family home has increased 70 percent since the bottom of 2012, with an average existing home now selling for $245,000 in southeast Wisconsin.[25] A basic analysis of supply and demand suggests that it is a great time for builders to build new houses, yet construction levels remain subdued. While there is certainly a need for new

housing stock, the constantly escalating costs of new construction have become an even greater challenge and have pushed
the affordability of a new home out of reach for many people.
New homes are approaching a price range of $150 to $200 per
square foot for a basic package; and this figure typically does
not include the land site. If you are in the market to buy a new
2,200-square-foot model home, the entry point is eclipsing
$450,000 for the package, which, even with historically low
interest rates, translates to around $3,000 per month.

To live on a financially responsible budget, a good rule of
thumb is to cap annual housing expenses (inclusive of principle,
interest, taxes, and insurance) at no more than 30 percent of
total gross income. The average Wisconsin middle-class house-
hold made $81,829 in 2020[26] so should spend no more than
$2,000 per month on housing. This clearly is not enough for the
$450,000 ($3,000/month) new house mentioned above. Using
the 30 percent rule, to justify the expense of a new $450,000
home, a family should be making at least $120,000 annually.

These numbers also expose the large gap in affordability
that has formed over the past decade. An annual income of
$120,000 is currently 45 percent higher than what the average
middle-class family in Wisconsin makes. What does housing
affordability mean for entry-level industrial labor in Wisconsin? Wage inflation has pushed starting pay in many industrial
operations to north of $18 per hour, or $40,000 per year. A single person in this wage range should be spending no more than
$1,000 per month on housing, and a couple should be spending
no more than $2,000 per month. The average family employed
in entry-level industrial operations in Wisconsin can afford

owning a $240,000 home. But, as noted above, the average existing home in Wisconsin now exceeds this price by $5,000, and new homes are nearly double that amount.

So, how do we make an impact and create more workforce housing alternatives for Wisconsin's middle class? The bulk of the cost of housing resides in material and labor. Both components have experienced ongoing cost pressures that are unlikely to abate given supply and demand constraints. The lumber panic of 2021 is a great example—not much we can do except let the free market figure it out. Land is the third leg of the cost stool. Supply and demand certainly play a significant role in driving the price of land, but the government also pulls a large lever. Government establishes zoning code, issues building permits, and determines how public infrastructure is delivered to a development. After all, unimproved land has little value outside of recreation or agriculture if the local government is not willing to facilitate development. I believe there is no better way to understand how to tackle this problem than by speaking to an industry leader.

Neumann Companies is one of the most reputable and successful residential real estate companies in the southern part of the state of Wisconsin. Four related residential development and home building companies operate under the Neumann flag, which, when combined, make up the second-largest group of building operators in the state. Its land development division, Neumann Development, is tasked with locating unimproved land sites, ushering the parcels through the approval and entitlement process, buying the land, and then improving the land. After this process is completed, one of its building company partners (Tim O'Brien Homes, Harbor Homes, or Halen Homes) takes over and builds single-family houses that are sold directly to the consumer. Harbor Homes is known for production style models that are both affordable and of high quality. These builders are consistently ranked as top metropolitan Milwaukee home builders for single-family units, and they delivered more than four hundred homes in 2021.

Neumann Companies was founded by Mark Neumann in 1979, and his son Matt is currently the second-generation owner and CEO. Very few operators possess the résumé and track record of Neumann in both land development *and* home construction. Over forty years of experience and developing over five thousand homesites and homes in more than fifty local municipalities also delivers a deep insight as to what drives root causes of industry trends. Matt provided me with a little historical context of the Milwaukee area residential market:

If you go back to the late 1940s, when the troops returned home from World War II, we had this massive build-out of single-family residences take place across Milwaukee, West Allis, and Wauwatosa. The expectations of the American people during this time frame were just different. Drive around the communities that were developed during this era and observe the housing stock. Houses had footprints of 800, 1,000, 1,200 square feet. A two-story home was often 1,400 square feet. Lot sizes were fifty feet wide with a thirty-foot-wide footprint for the house. Today, the average consumer wants at least double that footprint in a new home.

Before speaking to Matt, I had not heard the affordability debate focus on the reality that the consumer simply wants more. The cost of a new home is a basic multiplication problem: [the cost per square foot to build] x [the actual square footage] = [your price point]. If the consumer now demands a 2,400-square-foot home, the basis of the home is already double compared to what it would have been fifty to seventy years ago, without even considering the impacts of inflation. And there most certainly is inflation. With the cost of material and labor continuing to rapidly increase, a builder has limited options to contain costs.

MORE EQUALS LESS

Here is where zoning and land use come into the picture. An area that can drive down cost per unit is the level of scale achieved with total housing units in a development. Higher density presents much larger opportunities for scale. Most traditional suburban zoning promotes lots that reach up to one hundred feet or more in width. While many of us in Wisconsin love the concept of the perfectly manicured flush green yard, larger lots have led to larger home footprints. The practice of developing larger lot sizes also contributes to inefficient deployment of infrastructure coverage and substantially more infrastructure cost per homesite. The cost to service a development with infrastructure is roughly the same whether the subdivision has fifty homes or one hundred homes; the infrastructure is a fixed cost. But the one-hundred-lot subdivision can sell its lots at a lower price point than the fifty-lot subdivision because it can spread the infrastructure costs over double the number of lots. Matt provided me with a ballpark on southeast Wisconsin land prices as of October 2021. After infrastructure is delivered, a lot can sell for $1,500 per linear foot of frontage. Drop a seventy-foot lot to a fifty-foot lot, and the consumer can save $35,000. Denser subdivision development seems like a solution that would be widely adopted already by both communities and the consumer. Not so fast. Zoning came up several times in my conversation with Matt.

The local community and the consumer want it both ways when it comes to new housing development. Consumers want affordable options, but they also want bigger homes and lots. Many local community leaders believe affordable workforce housing is important, but they are reluctant to embrace zoning density. That begs the question: is the affordable housing discussion even focused on the correct problem? Matt has an interesting take on the conflicting objectives influencing housing policy. The focus on attaching the word "affordable" to new construction is misguided. "A conversation on how we get a $450,000 price point back under $300,000 is not productive. Our attention needs to be on how we drive that 450 number back down to 400." Matt then delivered my "aha moment" on the subject.

> Affordable workforce housing is actually the easing of the inventory stock of 800- to 1,500-square-foot homes that may be forty to sixty years old. By nature, a new home should carry a premium price to an existing home, but once the premium starts to eclipse 15

percent, the pool of potential buyers starts to dimin-
ish. The "new" premium is more than 60 percent right
now, which is keeping families locked into their existing $150,000 to $250,000 homes. The end result is a
market that continues to operate with limited housing
options in the "affordable" range.

Matt's statement on easing the inventory crunch at the
starter-home level gets to the core of the problem. New single-family homes aren't geared toward solving the affordability challenge, but new inventory is essential to help provide
trade-up options for growing families looking to move out of
the 1,200-square-foot West Allis bungalow.

Let's get back to the math challenges of delivering new
single-family residences. How do we drop the new baseline
of $450,000 down to $400,000? Local government leadership on zoning and land use is a critical component. On the
surface, many communities understand that offering a deeper
workforce housing mix for its residents is good long-term
public policy. Achieving actual results can be a much more
difficult process. Altering zoning codes and securing development approvals are a political process that can be subject
to the whims of a plan commission, a common council, or a
vocal neighborhood group. I will get into a couple of possible
solutions involving state-driven policy changes later in this
chapter, but leadership at the local level is perhaps the most
important component of delivering results in workforce housing. I believe businesses need to become much more engaged
within their communities, painting the picture of what can be

gained by providing more workforce housing stock. Politics at the local level can be conducted in a vacuum. Never underestimate the impact that a small, vocal group can make in the process, both positively and negatively.

Matt is somewhat optimistic that local communities will figure out solutions for how to grow their available housing stock. I asked Matt if he were governor for a day, what would be the two most impactful actions he would take with executive orders? He was quick to respond:

> Consistency in the interpretation of zoning law is absolutely critical for our business. Number one, I would require an update to the Smart Growth plans for every town, village, and city, and there would be an *obligation* to adhere to the plans they have ratified. Number two, communities would need to provide zoning ordinances that allow for the development of the ratified Smart Growth comprehensive plans. Zoning ordinances that match the desires laid out in the comprehensive master plans need to be an entitled right. Developers should not be subject to the whims of a PUD (planned unit development) process in order to develop a parcel of land that follows the community's comprehensive master plan.

I concluded my interview with Matt discussing the path that the state of Wisconsin needs to travel to become known as a national leader in workforce housing solutions by 2030. He reiterated, "The housing mix in 2030 needs to incorporate a full life cycle for our residents. We need to provide different price

points and different amenities from young adult to end of life."
Matt highlighted markets like Raleigh, North Carolina, which
have embraced fifty-foot lots and townhome-style developments that have exploded in popularity across major markets
in the United States. Neumann is delivering similar developments in the desirable communities of Sussex and Cedarburg
and, at the end of 2021, has been able to price a high-quality
1,800- to 2,000-square-foot detached single-family home for
$450,000. In solving a monumental challenge, framing the
problem with the proper perspective often holds the key to
taking the first step toward success.

I learned two profound insights from Matt. Number one,
local political leadership will be essential in driving the zoning changes needed to create more workforce housing options.
Number two, we need to reset the expectation that we can create affordable new "starter" homes. We can't. We can create
affordable new "next step" homes, which will lead to opening
up more existing starter-home inventory. Of all the opportunities to solve the labor shortage, I believe that providing workforce housing options presents the greatest potential to attract
and retain the middle-class families needed to fill our industrial jobs. Doing so is a SMART policy goal that Republicans
and Democrats can both agree on—a rare thing these days!

WORKFORCE HOUSING: CHANGING THE NARRATIVE

Public policy needs to drive Wisconsin's goal of being a
national leader in workforce housing solutions. As noted in the
previous section, local units of government play a significant

role in creating change, but we cannot overlook the potential impact that state policy can deliver as well. Two of the toughest challenges of creating new residential development are time to market and overall cost. Taking a project from an unimproved parcel to a new subdivision typically takes anywhere between one to three years of a developer's time. The approval process also can consume hundreds of thousands of dollars in soft costs that are spent on engineers, consultants, and attorneys. One unexpected turn can lead to a dead end and no project. Successful developers are astute at making calculated bets on the viability of a development at the front end. All the expended effort is for naught if they guess wrong.

Given the high-risk profile of land development, is there a way for state or local governments to provide prequalified opportunities that can be put into production immediately? I believe an opportunity does exist, and it can be modeled after the WEDC Certified Site program, launched in 2012 to better facilitate the pursuit of fast-tracked industrial and commercial business attraction efforts. Landowners (public or private) can enroll their sites in the program, which serves as a stamp of approval that the sites are ready for development. A Certified Site must meet the following criteria:

- Property title is clear.
- Sufficient utilities and other infrastructure for industrial use are run to the site.
- Environmental corridors and wetlands are delineated.
- Property is zoned and has adequate transportation access.

In my estimation, a Certified Site can accelerate the ground-breaking of a project by nine to eighteen months. Additionally, the upfront due diligence needed, such as zoning and wetland delineation, removes exposure to a substantial amount of soft costs. The program solves the two primary problems facing the development community, and it produces results. The community of Beloit was able to capture a one-thousand-job, one-million-square-foot Amazon development that opened in 2020 because they had a Certified Site ready to go in their Gateway Business Park.[27] The Certified Site designation stands out as a competitive differentiator for industrial development.

Many of the same principles that drive the success of the Certified Site program could be applied to a program for residential opportunities. The residential model could provide an efficient and structured approval process to ensure that a project can get out of the ground on a timely basis. Given its experience in housing policy, the Wisconsin Housing and Economic Development Authority (WHEDA) is best suited to oversee such a program. Much like the Certified Site program, enrolling would be up to the individual landowner or community. Pursuing the designation would benefit both parties; private landowners would enhance the value of their land by removing significant risk from the development, and the community would have a teed-up site ready for residential development, much like Beloit did for Amazon in the example above.

The following is a hypothetical concept for how the model could work:

1. Municipality targets an area of town in which they would like to spur the development of a new supply of dense, single-family lots.

2. Private property owner(s), or the municipality, enroll(s) the desired parcel(s) of land for fast-track development.

3. Industry-standard due diligence is performed up front, including a property survey, wetland delineation, environmental site assessment, and geotechnical review.

4. Municipality creates the desired unit yield for the development and establishes the appropriate zoning code.

5. Municipality specs out the needed infrastructure and develops a budget.

6. If the site is held by the municipality, the community offers up the development opportunity through a public process RFP (request for proposal) in which the community can establish the stated objectives of the development and select the best private-sector partner.

7. The community controls the amount of units to be delivered, the spec of the units, and the time frame for delivery, and they also can require the developer to share their return pro forma much like some TIF districts are turning to.

8. The developer starts building houses.

This unique approach can significantly reduce the land development risk assumed by a developer/builder and still allows for a preestablished profit margin, which will be needed to attract a quality development. In return, the community should be able to deliver cost savings for homesites and cut a meaningful amount of expense from the price of a new home.

BRING IN THE RESERVES

Perhaps the largest impediment to new development is the cost of infrastructure. The delivery of infrastructure to a development is the moment at which the idea becomes an actual project. Installation of sewer mains, water laterals, roads, and sidewalks has become incredibly expensive; in many cases, the cost to deliver infrastructure often exceeds the total value of the unimproved land. With much of the infrastructure expense being pushed onto the developer, many locations that could support new housing development simply never get off the ground given the upside-down economics.

TIF has proven to be the most successful economic development tool available at the local level. TIF's structure has many complexities, but to summarize at a very basic level, a community bonds up front to cover the costs incurred to prepare a site for development, such as installing infrastructure. The bonds are paid back by the real estate taxes that the new development generates over a period of up to twenty years. TIF is primarily targeted toward industrial and commercial development. As current law stands now, housing can qualify for TIF only in a mixed-use development and at no more than an allocation of 35 percent of the total development. This means that new single-family development has a very difficult time tapping into the powers of TIF.

One of the complexities to expanding the reach of TIF into residential development comes from the additional resources needed to fund residential development within a community. New residential development requires a host of additional services, most importantly the need for K–12 education. Given that TIF bonds are paid back through the property taxes generated from the development, and Wisconsin depends on property taxes at the local level to fund education, the funding challenges that could emerge from supercharging residential development through TIF are not too difficult to understand. Industrial expansions are typically light on community service needs, which makes diverting the property tax revenue to pay the bond service much more palatable. However, I believe that creating more opportunities to incorporate residential development into TIF structures has more upsides than downsides and that the state of Wisconsin should look at altering existing TIF law.

A handful of ideas could deliver immediate results. The most significant cost challenge in delivering new subdivision development is the expense of roads and utility infrastructure. Whether through TIF or a similar structure, the ability for a community to finance infrastructure for workforce housing developments would certainly help move the needle on market pricing. In addition to opening up TIF to single-family infrastructure, several other proposals to broaden the use of TIF in residential development are being discussed at the legislative level. Many of the suggested changes to current law would be more impactful at the multifamily level. The 35 percent housing cap in a mixed-use development has been proposed to be shifted to 60 percent, which would certainly add affordable apartments to mixed-use projects. Another TIF concept being floated would help accelerate the adaptive reuse of vacant office and commercial buildings into residences.

An existing program that is starting to be tapped more frequently allows for successful TIF districts to extend the district for one year and divert the tax increment to affordable housing developments. Under current state law, a TIF district (or "TID") that retires its debt and has paid off all its project costs can be extended for up to one year from the resolution date if the municipality uses the final year's increment to benefit affordable housing.[28] Milwaukee is a community that has successfully used this option. The money has been used to fund many of the programs within the city's Strong Neighborhoods Plan.[29] Simply extending the period to two years could double the resources available.

Relaxing residential restrictions in TIF law application and focusing on zoning, density, and infrastructure delivery would together send a very powerful message to Wisconsin communities, the message that they have access to the necessary tools needed to grow workforce housing options. Locals would still have complete control over their decisions surrounding growth. Several of these solutions might not get by without controversy. Before you take a position against more government assistance in single-family development, however, I would ask the question: is what we are doing now working? I point to the data and suggest it is not.

New-home supply is going down, and prices continue to go up. Keeping the potential resources of the government out of this conversation is fighting a fight with one hand tied behind our back. I want to stress that I am not advocating for central planning in which Madison decides where rows of workforce housing will be placed. Local communities should make the determination of who they want to be. If Kenosha wants to attract 1,500 new middle-class families by 2030 to fuel their industrial growth, it is up to their local politicians to adapt the land use and zoning code needed. Conversely, a community can opt *out* of attracting the people needed to grow an industrial base. State law often gets much of the attention, but I think most of the workforce housing challenges can be solved at the local level through zoning and density requirements. State government can change laws, specifically TIF legislation, to better facilitate the financing of residential development, but on its own, state law cannot change what residents demand of their communities. We know industrial employers need employees, and employers will move to communities that can provide access to them. But increasing access to workforce housing will take us only so far. Connecting Wisconsin through world-class infrastructure will deliver our economy to the next level of competitiveness.

CHAPTER 7

THE SPINE OF COMMERCE

> "The secret of change is to focus all of your energy not on fighting the old, but on building the new."
> —SOCRATES

INVESTING IN SLEEK, MODERN infrastructure is one of the least controversial public policy objectives discussed. Everyone loves the concept, but agreeing to the *types* of infrastructure needed and then getting it *built* is another matter. The Infrastructure Investment and Jobs Act of 2021 is a great example of the complexity of the topic. Of the $1.2 trillion package that was passed, $110 billion is allocated toward traditional infrastructure like roads and bridges. The balance of the package is scattered throughout an assortment of targeted areas such as broadband, electric vehicle charging stations, ports, and rail lines, to name a few.[30] By the way, it takes years for infrastructure projects to get permitted and built. Many of the investments approved in the act will not be delivered until later this decade. As then President Obama stated after the American

Recovery and Reinvestment Act, "Those shovel-ready jobs were not as shovel-ready as we expected." An economy like Wisconsin's, which is built on manufacturing, agriculture, and tourism, needs best-in-class infrastructure. Unfortunately, we are not there. The American Society of Civil Engineers provided Wisconsin with an overall grade of "C" in its 2020 infrastructure report card.[31]

Wisconsin is projected to receive more than $5.5 billion from the infrastructure act.[32] So what can we do with that? Before committing money to the wish lists of pet projects scattered throughout the state, we need to consider where the need of our infrastructure is taking us, not where we have been. Wisconsin possesses a unique set of challenges when it comes to efficient use of infrastructure coverage. We have seventy-two counties, ninety-nine assembly districts, and thirty-three senate districts, each with its own set of challenges and opportunities. Wisconsin's three largest counties (Milwaukee, Dane, and Waukesha) total approximately 1.9 million residents, or roughly 32 percent of the total population of the state. Contrast that with the population mass of the bottom three counties (Florence, Menomonee, and Iron) that have only 14,545 residents... *total*. The cost for a mile of road is roughly the same whether installed in Waukesha or Florence, but installing in Florence brings an exponential diminishing return on investment. More people equate to more usage, which drives economies of scale. This doesn't mean the road is any more important for the people in the Waukesha area than for those in the Florence area, but it does mean that in a world of limited resources, with structural deficits facing the transportation fund, the state of

Wisconsin would be best suited in taking a critical look at how we are selecting and funding projects.

I believe the state of Wisconsin would benefit most from developing a system that awards road construction projects based upon economic impact. The larger the economic impact, the more quickly a project should get built. As an example, the stretch of I-94 in Milwaukee County between the zoo and Marquette Interchanges (16th Street to 70th Street) is what I would classify as a maximum-impact project. The stretch is bookended by the reconstructed zoo and Marquette Interchanges and would amount to a substantial investment of over $1.2 billion for three and a half miles of freeway.[33] With a traffic volume of 160,000 vehicles per day, more than five hundred crashes per year, and being constructed over sixty years ago, this stretch of road is long overdue for a replacement. According to the Milwaukee Metropolitan Association of Commerce (MMAC), this section of freeway handles an estimated seventeen million tons of freight valued at $25 billion in economic activity. MMAC also states 21,000 businesses and 310,000 jobs are located within five miles of this corridor.[34] This is the type of project I hold up as one that should skip to the front of the line.

BUILDING WHERE THE GREATEST NEED IS

How do you objectively rank the economic impact of a road construction project? Create a ranking matrix and analyze the impacts of the project through a basic public benefit analysis. Some of the key factors in reviewing a new road project should include:

- Expected system load (vehicles per day and truck traffic)

- Crash history

- Traffic congestion

- Proximity to industry concentration

- Proximity to residents

The ranking system would inevitably benefit existing economic hub markets and would likely lead to delays, or even cancellations, of projects in outlier areas. Politically this concept will be difficult to accomplish, but as we look to use government resources more effectively, I believe we must start considering a return on investment when we are making massive financial commitments to projects. For those who doubt the multiplier effect of maximum-impact projects, you only need to drive and observe the twenty-six-mile stretch of Oak Creek to Pleasant Prairie that was recently upgraded to an eight-lane interstate. I want to emphasize *drive*, as the visual experience is far more impactful than any description I can provide.

Well-kept and easy-to-use roadway systems will continue to drive industrial growth throughout the key areas of the state. I referenced the ongoing structural deficits Wisconsin will continue to face over the coming decade. The shortfall already has put us in a position of delaying or canceling key projects, such as the 94 East–West. The economic ranking impact is a potential path to sustaining key investments in the projects that truly move the needle, but some communities will be winners and some will be losers.

If we cannot overcome the politics of outlier areas losing funding for road projects, then I believe the math is quite clear: we will need to raise revenues. Costs keep going up, but options to raise revenue have remained limited. While popular for the consumer, Wisconsin's gas tax has been fixed since 2006, and we derive nearly 50 percent of our annual transportation budget from the gas tax.[35] Recent budget negotiations have not produced a path to increasing the gas tax; instead lawmakers have turned to an assortment of fee increases on title transfers and vehicle registration to help backfill some of the gap; however, these options have barely put a dent in the problem.

Funding challenges at the Department of Transportation level are not unique to Wisconsin. Since 2013, thirty-three states have moved to increase their gas taxes.[36] The gas tax typically provides a stable source of revenue and is also a true user fee. You are only paying the tax if you are putting gas in your vehicle and driving. This seems like a fair proposition to me. But an increase in the gas tax is also one of the most noticeable impacts to the consumer, especially in a time like 2022, when gas prices soared past four dollars per gallon. The additional challenge to increasing dependency on gas tax revenue is the accelerating wave of the movement to electric vehicles. If you are not pumping gas, you are not paying the tax.

While the politics of solving the funding challenges will not be easy, some of the solutions are not that complex, either. I believe these three ideas can be impactful:

- The gas tax is one of the simplest user fees to assess and has been fixed since 2006. If we need to increase revenues, the gas tax needs to be on the table.

- E-tolling, especially for visitors from out of state, should be a no-brainer. Why should we place user fee increases exclusively onto the backs of Wisconsin residents?

- Electric vehicles need to be assessed user fees in some manner to offset the pending collapse in gas consumption. This could be an annual fee, mileage fee, or even a sales tax on electrical consumption attributed to vehicle charging.

A network of well-maintained and accessible roads is a necessity for the state of Wisconsin's industrial economy. The current state of the debate needs to move beyond the incremental approach of a patchwork of nominal fees designed to keep the status quo afloat for another biennium budget cycle. We need to both judge projects based upon a projected return on investment and change the way we are funding them.

GETTING PEOPLE TO JOBS

Driving your car down a smooth road without potholes or congestion delays is likely the first thing that comes to mind when you hear the word infrastructure. Maintaining a sleek, modern network of roads is a must-have if we want to efficiently move people and products throughout the state. But is delivering best-in-class roads enough for our employers? Are we missing out on a golden opportunity if we do not have a supporting plan to increase connectivity between workers and employers? The demand for workers has created a sense of urgency around figuring out better ways to get people to jobs. Given the tightness of the labor market, we cannot afford to leave people out of the workforce simply because they do not have access to an automobile. Many companies have waded into this discussion, yet solutions to increase connectivity remain elusive. Mass transit sounds good in theory, but in my opinion, Wisconsin's geography is not set up to capitalize on the potential benefits of mass transit. I see two primary challenges:

- Commute times are not an issue for most Wisconsinites. An Armageddon traffic event in the Milwaukee area would rarely create a commute time of more than sixty minutes to get from one end of town to the other. It is much faster for a person to use an automobile than to ride transit.

- Successful transit systems typically need density, and Wisconsin's population hubs are far too spread out. Primary population centers, such as Milwaukee, Madison, and Green Bay, are separated by more than ninety minutes and eighty miles.

The Milwaukee area proves to be a prime example of the difficulties of connecting inner-city residents with suburban jobs. Regional leaders generally agree that many jobs need to be filled in the suburbs and that a dense pool of job candidates is available in the city of Milwaukee. One would think this dynamic would naturally lead to much better success in connecting the dots, but little progress is being made. The situation feels like two ships passing in the night. Why is this happening? I would point to the two main challenges that I noted above: time and distance. A thirty-minute one-way travel time is about as far as most of the blue-collar workforce will consider for a commute time. After that, the concept of time and money comes into play. Bus transit might be the only transportation alternative available for a worker, but a traditional bus route, with multiple stops along the way, can add significant time to a commute. Thirty minutes in a car can quickly become sixty minutes on a bus. If we are to find a sustainable solution in connecting more people to jobs, we need to confront the reality of commute times. Very few people are interested in riding on a bus for two hours per day when they are making less than $30,000 per year. Put yourself in that position—would you spend that amount of time riding the bus for less than fifteen dollars per hour?

How do we know this thirty-minute paradox to be true? The Public Policy Forum released one of the best research pieces I have read on the topic entitled *Getting to Work*. It highlighted the one-way travel times between Brookfield Square and four zip codes facing higher unemployment in Milwaukee County. The quickest commute on a Monday morning was fifty-seven minutes.[37] There have been several attempts to establish bus connections into Waukesha County over the past couple of decades, most recently with two routes that serviced job centers in New Berlin and Menomonee Falls. Both options were funded through a lawsuit settlement that came out of the expansion of the Zoo Interchange. The 2014 settlement established $13.5 million of dedicated funding to support two years of expense for the routes, and the ACLU lauded the funding as a "landmark victory" that would enhance job opportunities for inner-city workers.[38] Despite high expectations for the routes, given the density of employers in the designated service area, ridership never materialized for either route. The route to New Berlin was discontinued at the end of 2018, and the route entering Menomonee Falls was significantly reconfigured and scaled back because most of the ridership for the route was using the service only to commute between stops within City of Milwaukee limits.[39] Time and time again we see that people are not interested in sitting in transit for more than an hour a day.

What can be done to increase the speed of service? Attempts are being made to develop bus rapid transit (BRT) lines along dedicated routes in the Milwaukee area. The initial BRT line under construction will run from downtown Milwaukee to the Medical Research Center in Wauwatosa, with eventual plans to extend to Waukesha.

A dedicated bus line along a major commercial corridor is a step in the right direction; however, the line still possesses *seventeen* stations. To reduce commute times on a bus, the number of stops needs to be reduced and routes need to remain on straight lines as much as possible. Effective mass transit in the Milwaukee area also must address the last-mile problem. The hub-and-spoke approach of delivering workers from drop-off points to the front door of businesses becomes essential. The state of Wisconsin most certainly could play a role in facilitating grants or tax credits for participating companies, but I believe the last-mile solution is best suited for private businesses to figure out. Whether this is through direct shuttle van transportation fleets owned and operated by businesses, rideshare models, or pooled resources of an industrial park association, too many variables must be accounted for that require the nimbleness of the private sector.

Identifying how to get more candidates to your place of business is a strategic advantage. If you need people, you need to find where they are, and you need to be able to get them to your door. This is easier said than done; operating a hub-and-spoke model to deliver workers creates its own unique set of challenges. Going back to the concept of time and money when delivering mass transit in Wisconsin, the reality facing our state is that using a personal vehicle is reasonably cheap and saves significant time. So, what happens when entry-level workers who use the transit system transition into long-term employees and experience their first pay raises? They typically want to get off the bus and buy their own automobiles.

BROADBAND

Access to high-speed internet connectivity is no longer a "nice-to-have" for Wisconsin residents and businesses. It is a *must-have*. The pandemic taught us that the state was not quite ready to flip the switch to the virtual world. According to the 2021 Broadband Deployment Report by the Federal Communications Commission (FCC), roughly 394,900 people in Wisconsin lack access to high-speed broadband service, defined as a service with speeds of twenty-five megabits per second (Mbps) download and three Mbps upload (25/3 Mbps).[40] The study also found that Wisconsin ranks thirty-sixth nationwide for broadband access in rural areas, with 21.8 percent of residents being noted as unserved or underserved. The rural disconnect is a big deal for our state.

In my opinion, broadband policies should target three distinct camps: the individual consumer, education and healthcare, and operating businesses and agriculture. While I am not discounting the importance of the first two groups, my interest is in business and agriculture. Specifically, where are the opportunities to improve dependability and speed throughout our network, and how are we evaluating the return on investment?

The multiple COVID-19 rescue packages passed since the onset of the pandemic have allocated billions of dollars toward increasing broadband connectivity throughout the United States. The federal government primed the pump with massive financial support to assist with the rollout of increased broadband service, especially in rural areas. But what does this mean for Wisconsin? From 2014 through 2021, Wisconsin received federal commitments of roughly $1.45 billion to expand broadband.[41] Additionally, the 2021 Infrastructure Investment and Jobs Act is expected to send us another $100 million in funding.[42] With a solid base of seed funding from the feds, what progress are we making? Governor Evers convened a broadband task force in 2020 that produced a comprehensive report of broadband recommendations moving forward. The sixty-two-page report[43] was compiled by a task force of twenty-six public and private sector leaders, and specific goals were established as follows:

MEASURABLE ACCESS

- By 2025 all homes and businesses will have access to 25/3 Mbps speeds.

- By 2028 all homes and businesses will reach 50/10 Mbps speeds.

- By 2031 all homes and businesses will reach 100/50 Mbps speeds.

MEASURABLE CAPACITY

- By 2025 50 percent of homes and businesses will have access to one gigabit per second (Gbps) of speed.

- By 2030 90 percent of homes and businesses will have access to one Gbps of speed.

The report serves as an excellent starting point but does not cover much in suggesting the projected costs to deliver the stated goals. As an example, the state's 2020–2021 biennium budget invested $125 million toward the build-out of broadband, and understanding how this amount will help move the needle on the task force's goals would be helpful. Does it get us to 50 percent of the goal or 5 percent? Comprehending the total cost projections to fully build out a network becomes essential for reviewing any infrastructure project. The goal of serving all homes and businesses sounds great, but is it financially feasible?

I believe connecting Wisconsin's rural manufacturers and farms needs to be a top priority of Wisconsin's ten-year broadband plan. Connectivity for a rural business user will look a lot

different than a traditional service that can deliver an uninterrupted Netflix series.

Let's start with where both the industries of manufacturing
and agriculture are headed: the Internet of Things (IoT). Much
of the broadband conversation to date has surrounded simple
delivery speed, e.g., how quickly can I get online and download
emails? I do not believe this is the problem we need to be solving. As technology continues to develop, a simple connection is
no longer enough. The future of business will require multiple
devices communicating in real time in the cloud, which will
lead to the processing of impactful data points and real-time
predictive analytics that support proactive decision-making.

This sounds futuristic, but the opportunities are already
here. John Deere is manufacturing agricultural equipment with
cloud-based capabilities to assist farmers with a data-driven
approach to planting and harvesting crops. If the tools are used
appropriately, the result is a more bountiful harvest with less
manpower. Manufacturers now have the capability to operate
fully automated lines across multiple plants that can all be
connected through the cloud and can sync cross-functionally
in real time. Again, this provides more output with less labor,
but getting to this level requires a significant amount of speed
and capacity in a telecommunications network. The challenge
in rural Wisconsin is that we do not have the infrastructure
in place to facilitate the connections. Possessing cutting-edge
technology means nothing if we do not have access to the back
engine to power it.

I view the public–private partnership model as the most
effective way to rapidly build out the needed rural networks.

Much like my proposal for road funding, I believe that rural projects should be reviewed through an economic impact application. The process could be as follows:

1. A local business works with a network contractor to create an application for funding.

2. An application is submitted to a local unit of government, which acts as facilitator of the grant process and administrator of the grant funding.

3. The local unit of government submits the application to the state, and the state has a sixty-day window to review and approve or reject the application. If approved, the state transfers the requested funds to the local unit of government, which then disperses the funds to the network contractor.

Ultimately, the state of Wisconsin must take decisive action on what it wants its rural economy to look like. Time is not on our side. If we cannot rapidly advance the connectivity service offerings needed to compete and win in modern manufacturing and agriculture, much of our rural economy will continue down the path of becoming totally dependent on recreation and tourism.

POWER

Modern industrial development also requires a dependable and affordable utility grid.

I place available energy in the "absolute necessity" bucket. A development site must have access to the necessary electrical

and gas service that an end user will need, or the site is immediately eliminated from consideration. Electricity is somewhat
of a commodity, so the differentiation of product offering is
determined by capacity, distribution, and rates. Wisconsin is
a regulated utility state in which a single-service provider controls a territory, and the public service commission (PSC) sets
pricing. Proponents would suggest a regulated utility provides
for predictable pricing and a much more reliable grid that can
sustain shocks to the system, specifically, natural disasters.
Opponents would suggest that regulated energy markets are
just another name for a monopoly and that lack of competition leads to higher prices and, more importantly, to no choice
for the consumer. Presently, twenty-six states operate with all
or partial deregulation of electricity and gas.[44] Wisconsin and
Minnesota happen to be the only two Great Lakes states that
remain regulated. This topic is rather controversial, quite complex, and inherently political.

Energy consumption is one of the single largest line-item
expenses for manufacturing operations. Wisconsin is perceived
as an expensive utility state, which is not a great selling point
when recruiting industrial expansions. As of September 2021,
Wisconsin had the highest electrical rates in the East North
Central Region of the country with an average industrial user
rate of 8.18 cents per kilowatt hour (kWh) versus 6.85 to 7.85
cents per kWh for our neighbors. Iowa had one of the lowest
rates in the country at 6.06 cents per kWh, which is nearly 25
percent lower than ours.[45] Large manufacturers can spend millions of dollars per year on energy, and even a 5 percent swing
can have a big impact on their bottom lines.

Total cost has traditionally been the primary driver of utility consideration for an end user; however, recent natural disaster events have made dependability of service more of a priority than ever before. Continual wildfire outbreaks in California and the Texas deep freeze of 2021 exposed significant flaws in the electrical grids of both states. Wisconsin boasts of a dependable and secure grid, and we do have a geographic advantage as it relates to the likelihood of sustaining a natural disaster event. Outside of an occasional tornado, we have very few natural disaster impacts to be concerned about.

The state also has displayed the capacity and wherewithal to react quickly to expand service for economic development opportunities. The Foxconn development required a $140-million upgrade to local utility service, which delivered 230 megawatts of capacity to the grid. The service was swiftly approved by the PSC, an impressive feat given that the upgrade was more than six times the load of Wisconsin's then largest manufacturer.[46]

But at the end of the day, electricity is an operating expense just like property taxes, and if our neighbors are beating us, we need to pay attention. The Wisconsin Industrial Energy Group (WIEG) provides some of the best private-industry thought leadership on this topic. WIEG is composed of twenty-five of the heaviest electrical users in the state who spend over $400 million annually on electricity and employ over fifty thousand Wisconsin residents.[47] WIEG's website offers the following statement: "WIEG's efforts in the drafting of legislation and administrative rules, and its participation in utility construction cases, base rate cases and fuel cases, has resulted in very substantial energy cost savings for member companies. *In the last ten years, investor-owned utility rate hike requests have been reduced by roughly 69 percent for a total of over $1.3 billion.*" If you take the time to review WIEG's 2022 policy positions, you will quickly understand that cost is the number one challenge facing its members.

I predict industrial users will give much greater consideration to the dependability of the local energy grid over the coming decade. Far too many recent events across the country have led to extended power outages. Wisconsin should stack up rather well in this category, but possibly not enough. We need to take note when our largest manufacturers continually lament about how difficult investing in Wisconsin is, given the high expense of electricity. If we are looking to capture more expansion opportunities from manufacturers, we need to both emphasize the resiliency of our grid and set a goal of moving the cost into the top ten least expensive states in the country.

WATER

Fresh water is a feature that presents a unique advantage for the state, especially for communities within the Lake Michigan watershed. As the world continues to grapple with growing populations and erratic climate swings, access to clean and fresh water is controlled by nothing more than geography. A region either has access to a bulk water supply for industrial users or it does not. The Great Lakes region likely will receive much more attention in the coming years from businesses that use water for their processes.

Over the past decade, southeast Wisconsin has set out to brand itself as the freshwater capital of the world. As noted earlier in the book, the Water Council was officially formed in 2009 to shine a light on the vast number of companies based in the Milwaukee area involved in any industry that touches water. Currently, the council consists of 255 companies, and the roster contains several global market leaders such as A. O. Smith, Zurn, and Badger Meter. An additional part of the strategy is to properly align talent resources needed to support advanced research. The UW-Milwaukee School of Freshwater Sciences subsequently opened in 2014 and is the only program in the United States dedicated to the study of fresh water. We have the companies and the institutional knowledge to lead the world in any industry that touches water.

One year prior to the formation of the Water Council, the ratification of the 2008 Great Lakes Water Compact further cemented our freshwater advantage. The pact effectively shut down any prospect of exporting Great Lakes water outside of the Great Lakes watershed. Access to fresh water was a critical recruiting tool for the initial iteration of the Foxconn project. The process of manufacturing electronics requires a substantial amount of freshwater and wastewater treatment, and the available water supply in the Great Lakes region was a key component in the site selection review. Mount Pleasant and Racine County were able to work within the confines of the Great Lakes compact, and they successfully received authorization to divert up to seven million gallons of water per day from Lake Michigan to service the proposed development. At the time, the accessibility to the volume of water needed to service the project was a true differentiator for the region and was considered a key factor in winning the deal.

To date, I do not believe that access to fresh water has been a driving force in site selection, but that might be changing in the not-too-distant future. When building a plant in the United States, clean and available water is considered a given. But that assumption can no longer be taken for granted in many states like California, Nevada, and Arizona. Areas that have limited access to fresh water might find themselves boxed out of new growth opportunities. And because of supply and demand, water is something we do not have to give away, either. If you need access to water, you need to account for what is becoming a fixed and limited supply. Locating within the Great Lakes Watershed and the state of Wisconsin is a distinct value proposition. What are some of the industries to watch for? Semiconductor and pharmaceuticals could be huge opportunities for the region, especially on the heels of the great supply chain reset of 2021. Other areas Wisconsin could compete favorably in are food and beverage, automotive, plastics, and paper and pulp—all industries in which Wisconsin has background and expertise.

Providing a deep pool of skilled workers along with world-class infrastructure *almost* gets us to where we need to be. Many modern-day economic development pursuits need that final extra incentive to push them over the top.

CHAPTER 8

PLAY TO WIN

"Underdog strategies are hard."
—MALCOLM GLADWELL

FOR MANY SIGNIFICANT site-selection projects, an offering of a lucrative incentive package is typically an expectation of doing a deal—a state's price of entry to enter the corporate site selection sweepstakes. State and local governments are pitted against each other to drive up the total purse available for the end user, and to the winner goes the spoils. An attractive incentive package can serve as the cherry on top of the sundae to close the deal, but companies need to check the box on many other factors before incentives truly start to matter. As sizable as Wisconsin's offering to Foxconn was, credible rumors indicated that the state was not even the highest bidder.[48] In a close race, incentives might put you over the top, but a package on its own will not keep you running long enough to have the chance to win.

The topic of incentives does not come without controversy (which I will cover in greater detail later in this chapter). The reality is that Wisconsin competes against forty-nine other states for economic development, and the use of incentives does factor into the decision-making process of the C-suite. Some states consistently perform very well in the Fortune 500 recruiting game. Texas is a great example of a corporate recruiting juggernaut given its low tax regime, excellent location, and growing population. Wisconsin is not known as one of the more aggressive states when it comes to incentives. Frankly, before Foxconn, we really weren't even in the game.

One of the most powerful tools a state can offer to an end user is extended property tax abatement. Wisconsin cannot offer this benefit. We are constitutionally bound by the uniformity clause, which requires that all properties, from residential to industrial, are taxed according to a fair market value. This clause takes a powerful tool off the incentive table. As an example, Wisconsin was a finalist for a massive Intel chip plant development pursued throughout 2021. Intel ultimately decided on a site in New Albany, Ohio, a suburb of the Columbus area. New Albany was able to offer a 100 percent property tax abatement on the value of the buildings for a thirty-year period.[49]

Wisconsin turns to two primary tools for economic development pursuits: tax increment financing (TIF), which is run through the local level, and the Business Development Tax Credit Program, which is administered through the Wisconsin Economic Development Corporation. If a large incentive package is being discussed, it is likely that both options are working in tandem. As I have noted earlier in this book, I believe Wisconsin's best opportunities to grow its industrial base come from its homegrown companies. I am not an advocate for going all in on the incentives game to lure out-of-state companies because I do not believe it aligns with how we have historically grown our economy. That stated, if we are going to remain dependent upon TIF and tax credits to support business growth, I do believe opportunities exist to improve the offerings and better align the process for both the private sector (who is creating the economic impact) and the public (who is funding the incentives).

TIF is the most powerful economic development tool a local community can turn to when pursuing new commercial and industrial development. In the *Building the Right Answer* chapter, I touched upon a simplistic explanation of how a community can utilize TIF to support real estate development. The tool was originally designed to assist with costs associated with infrastructure, site preparation, blight, and environmental remediation, but additional buckets such as developer incentives and cash grants have been added over time. For a TIF to be approved, it needs to pass a but-for test, meaning dollars cannot be allocated unless the development cannot proceed "but for" the financial assistance that the TIF would provide. As project costs continue to mount, turning to TIF to solve for financial gaps has become the norm for most new development, so much so that an alliance of politicians from both the left and the right have targeted potential legislation to limit the use of the tool.

TIF has been instrumental in kick-starting many large business parks across the state. Accounting firm Baker Tilly produced one of the best research pieces on the benefits of TIF. It found that for every one dollar invested in a TIF district, the return on investment was an additional $4.66 in new tax base.[50]

The use of TIF has evolved since first introduced in 1975. Many early TIF developments front-loaded the delivery of substantial fixed infrastructure, typically not knowing who the end user(s) was going to be. "Build it and they will come" was the philosophy. This can be a very effective way to spur development, but this model carries much more risk for a community because the end user demand might not materialize.

Communities have become much more educated and creative in protecting against downside risks. Concepts such as developer/user guarantees, or a Pay-Go TIF, have become quite popular. The Foxconn development is a great example of a guaranteed TIF. Nearly $1 billion of bonding was issued by Mount Pleasant to deliver the infrastructure for the area and to acquire the land. As part of the negotiation, Foxconn agreed to a minimum assessed value of $1.4 billion for its real estate holdings and a guaranteed annual property tax payment starting in 2023 of $27.4 million.[51] This amount was enough to pay the debt service on the bonds. With the security of a corporate guarantee, the community was able to front a substantial investment that opened up thousands of additional acres for development.

Pay-Go also has proven to be a successful model when looking to mitigate public risks. The bonding is once again guaranteed by an end user, and the public incentive is paid back to the end user over time through the annual property taxes generated by the development. Upon the municipality receiving the annual property tax payment, a refund is issued to the end user. Each Pay-Go agreement is subject to negotiation, with the most common agreements lasting between ten to fifteen years and the end user receiving 50 percent to 75 percent of the annual property tax payment as a rebate. This model ensures the public incentive is paid out only when the end user delivers on what was promised. It is a win–win for both private and public interests and significantly drops the risk for the community.

The use of the developer's incentive, or cash grant bucket, has become more and more popular within a TIF and adds a much greater degree of flexibility to add firepower to the offering. As an example, an existing vacant building located in a TIF district could require significant renovations for an interested manufacturer. The completed renovations and new tenant will increase the tax assessed value of the property, a key qualifier for the application of TIF. The property owner or tenant will have to guarantee an increased assessed value of the building, but this scenario could qualify for a cash grant incentive. While certainly outside the boundaries of the original legislation, the additional applications can lead to a make-or-break incentive offering for an expansion.

Two primary changes could be incorporated into TIF law to further increase its impact on industrial development. Current law applies a 12 percent cap on the total amount of tax assessed value a community can carry under an active TIF. Moving to a 15 percent cap is a reasonable solution that will continue to allow for prodevelopment policies in mature communities that might have reached their TIF limits. This change is even more important for cities that have tapped out their available supply of developable land and need to turn to much more costly redevelopment opportunities to grow their tax bases.

An additional change I would pursue is allowing for an industrial TIF to extend to a life of thirty years, which was accomplished with special legislation for the Foxconn development. As the size and scale of new industrial construction has grown, the costs of the needed infrastructure to service the development continue to put pressure on the current maximum payback period of twenty-three years. The Intel deal noted above leveraged a new state of Ohio budget provision that allowed for double the length of the property tax abatement period from fifteen years to thirty.

THE NEXT LEVEL

While incentives are not the calling card of Wisconsin, we have proven that we can compete when needed. The Business Development Tax Credit is the most powerful incentive tool at the state level. The program is administered through WEDC and touches four key areas:

1. Job Creation: up to a 10 percent credit for new jobs created for wages up to $100,000

2. Training: up to 50 percent of the eligible training costs incurred to enhance skills

3. Capital Investment: up to 3 percent of personal property and 5 percent of real property investment for projects worth at least $1 million

4. Corporate Headquarters: location or retention, up to 10 percent of total wages (up to $100,000) of positions created or retained[52]

One of the key qualifiers for the program is that Wisconsin needs to compete for the investment with one or more out-of-state locations. The term "compete" is used very loosely. An existing occupier in the state need merely suggest the investment can occur anywhere outside of Wisconsin to check this box, even if there is a 0 percent chance that a relocation is under consideration. I think this requirement often creates a concocted story line that provides little to no value for either the state or the end occupier. While I understand local communities can be sensitive to the state potentially incentivizing a company to relocate to a neighboring community, we need to get beyond the local politics of where economic development occurs—just as long as it happens in Wisconsin.

The current tax credit system also is geared toward helping big businesses over small businesses. This is especially true when a qualifier for incentives requires the threat of relocation. While large companies with footprints around the globe can make a legitimate claim that they can take the investment anywhere, this is not the case for small- to medium-sized companies with a single location in Wisconsin. A privately held business in a small town cannot casually (or credibly) state it is prepared to move to a different region. In its present form, the Business Development Tax Credit effectively boxes out WEDC's ability to assist small industrial businesses with growth opportunities. If I could change one thing about the current program, it would be to find ways to drop some of the qualifiers like "credible threat" and "corporate headquarters" and to make the awards more dependent on targeted growth industries, such as advanced manufacturing, automation, and food and beverage. This would open up awards to some of the businesses that need help the most, privately held companies that do not have access to the available capital that many of the large occupiers can tap into. If we want to grow our own, we need to give them the fuel.

One additional thought on incentives: make sure you know what you are signing up for. As companies espouse the values of social responsibility, incentives must be reviewed through the additional prism of long-term public perception impacted by our politics. When local or state governments are involved with providing incentives, the pride and joy of a ribbon-cutting ceremony can vanish at the first signs of trouble. Growing a new workforce is difficult enough without having to fight local media and 50 percent of the state residents that might oppose the governing party that provided the incentive package. An excellent example is the Foxconn incentive award I previously discussed. The Foxconn deal became a key wedge issue in the 2018 Wisconsin governor's race within months of the package being approved. The public backlash helped swing the governor's race to the challenger Tony Evers, and it also handed Foxconn a big black eye with half of the state's population before it could even open its doors. I believe when negotiating an incentives agreement, two critical components are necessary to create a successful public and private partnership for the deal:

1. Contingent tax credit awards should be the new model moving forward. If public money is involved, doing what you say you are going to do needs to be the key to receiving the incentive package being offered. Business plans can change rapidly, and the ability to pivot within an agreement is more important than ever.

2. TIF outlays need to position a community for future success. The big win for Mount Pleasant in the Foxconn deal was the infrastructure delivered to a wide swath of the community, and this area is now attracting commercial and residential development unrelated to Foxconn.

Unless all fifty states vote to ban the use of incentives, incentives will continue to play a role in the site selection decision-making process. Wisconsin does not need to be the most lavish spender in the incentives game to compete, but we do need to be one of the smartest and most deliberate. We have little margin for error when competing for mega projects against the likes of Texas and Ohio. While we should not forego the opportunity to occasionally pursue the home-run deal, I believe we will be much further ahead at the end of this decade by consistently hitting singles and doubles. And as we continue to hit our singles and doubles, the companies that choose to expand in Wisconsin are going to need new factories and warehouses to grow into.

CHAPTER 9

THE NEW INDUSTRIAL FRONTIER

PEOPLE SELECT THE PLACE they want to live based upon the unique characteristics of a community. Certain attributes instantly come to mind just hearing some communities' names. What are the first images that pop in your mind when you hear Madison? Wausau? Green Bay? Brookfield? Long-range community planning is extremely important in establishing the development priorities of a city, village, or town. Thoughtful planning preserves the character of an area and sets the path for future growth. One of the most significant challenges communities face in managing their future growth is balancing an existing well-thought-out comprehensive plan with an abrupt shift in market conditions. Commercial real estate development is a cyclical business, and each vertical (industrial, office, retail, medical, and multifamily) is prone to volatile market swings influenced by factors completely out of anyone's control. COVID's impact on the need for office space is a great example.

While I love observing a construction site for a new industrial building and seeing precast concrete walls being tilted up,

I appreciate that industrial real estate does not present the most desirable development outcome for the needs of some communities. It remains to be seen if the pandemic has permanently or temporarily shifted human behaviors on how people work in an office and shop in a store. We are living in a real-time social experiment, and the answers we realize over the coming years will determine the future wave of many commercial developments. In the interim, office and retail developments will face headwinds.

Selective opportunities for new projects will continue to be available in both categories; however, the pace that we have come to expect over the past several decades will likely disappoint.

When I started in the commercial real estate business in 2000, shopping centers, regional malls, and big-box stores were proliferating across America. Retail was *the* real estate vertical everyone wanted to get into. In a twist of good luck that I would not realize for about fifteen years postgraduation, I missed out on not one but two internships that would have placed me on the retail brokerage track. Industrial and retail are unrecognizable compared to where these segments were positioned two short decades ago. The past five years in particular have fundamentally altered how the two verticals operate. Traditional retailers like Kohl's had been trudging through a difficult transition period throughout the 2010s as e-commerce incrementally chipped away at the past dominance of brick-and-mortar stores. Then the pandemic hit, and the world changed...overnight. Society as we knew it was shut down, and retailers were forced to adapt to a world in which consumers mass-migrated to e-commerce and delivery services. With millions of new customers exposed to the simplicity of ordering online, the use of industrial real estate was significantly changed in one short year.

Many retail shops were deemed "nonessential," restaurants closed, and the physical office transitioned to the virtual world of Zoom, yet industrial operations were open for business. Warehouses and factories remained beehives of activity—but there was a problem making the honey. Companies were caught flat-footed as they could not get product from their overseas suppliers and container ships were stuck in ports for weeks. Online orders and supply chain challenges created an environment of unprecedented demand for industrial space. Inventory management needed to move from "just in time" to "just in case" to keep up with the demand volatility in the market. A renewed focus on investing in domestic capacity and capabilities followed suit, and the Decade of Industrial was born.

New industrial buildings continued to grow in size and the investment capital followed. Investor dollars rushed out of office and retail assets and poured into industrial real estate as a safe-haven investment. The surge of investment capital is important to note because a large portion of the industrial real estate supply pipeline is being constructed as speculative development; that is, constructing buildings without tenants already lined up to occupy them. This type of development requires a significant amount of capital, both on the equity and debt side. The flow of money into industrial real estate has created nearly unlimited liquidity for experienced developers, and we are experiencing a record surge of development because of this dynamic. Why is this important?

A community possessing inventory of speculative buildings has a competitive advantage in attracting industrial growth given the tight time frames that many companies are operating under as we emerge from the pandemic. Decisions on expanding capacity have been reduced to months, which means a company must have access to a stock of existing vacant buildings if they want to take advantage of changing market conditions. Spec buildings also immediately add a property tax base, but this doesn't mean there should be a free-for-all. Despite the property tax revenue, communities do not want a wave of unoccupied warehouses sprouting up all over town. Extensive vacant properties can be a drag on overall property values by creating the perception of a challenged area. A balance must be maintained. To keep a sustainable pace of development moving, the market needs companies to occupy the buildings. One of the greatest surprises brought on by the pandemic is the insatiable *user* demand for warehouse space. Industrial companies across the United States can not lease enough of it. Here at home, the Milwaukee 7 Region more than doubled its record year of space absorption in 2021 with more than fourteen million square feet of new space occupied in one calendar year. To put that in perspective, that amount is 5 percent of the total industrial stock in the region.[53] This phenomenon also appears to be more than a one-year wonder. The wave has legs, and many are predicting that this run could last for several more years. Prominent industrial real estate firms such as JLL are predicting that e-commerce alone could drive the need for one billion square feet of new warehouse space across the United States by 2025.[54]

A speculative warehouse building doesn't really get people all that excited, but it creates substantial property taxes for a community. A new two-hundred-thousand-square-foot industrial building will likely carry an assessed value of $13 million or more. This equates to roughly $260,000 in annual property tax revenue for your average village or city. Racine County offers up an excellent real-life example of the profound impact that industrial development is delivering at the local level. The past five years have produced over 3.75 million square feet of brand-new industrial space, and that total excludes the Foxconn development. When fully assessed, the property values of the new industrial developments should approach $225 million and deliver close to $5 million in annual property tax revenue. With industrial vacancy rates seemingly achieving new record lows on a quarterly basis, developers and businesses will have to keep building new industrial buildings. The M7 Region could easily add five million square feet per year for the extended future, which equates to roughly $325 million in added property tax base each and every year.

I get it; industrial is still not as sexy as the gleaming new high-tech campus, but communities are going to have to come to terms that industrial development is likely going to be the most active sector in commercial real estate for several years to come. Communities who do not change with the times will suffer consequences. A property tax reform package that dates to 2011 established that communities can increase their total tax levy limits only by the annual growth rate in new construction or by passing a local referendum. This reform has proven to be quite successful in holding property taxes in check and is popular with property owners, but many municipalities continue to face revenue challenges given the handcuffs. This model encourages communities to grow their tax base or fall behind. Industrial real estate is positioned with the clearest runway for growth and value appreciation over the coming decade, and communities that choose to embrace industrial real estate will be able to keep tax revenues flowing into their coffers.

THE COMING DECADE

As we power through the Decade of Industrial, communities will need to consider three significant challenges and opportunities as they look to attract new development:

1. Desire for large parcels of industrial land has created a developer rush on sites located within close access to major highway systems and population centers.

2. Same-day delivery is now the expectation of all e-commerce providers. This has led to a surge of demand for industrial real estate from companies that only three years ago would have never even thought of taking on a warehouse in Wisconsin.

3. E-commerce creates larger volumes of truck and van traffic. The goods we order online need to get to our door somehow; logistics operations use semi trucks to get goods to their warehouses and delivery vehicles to drop packages on doorsteps.

I believe the entire debate of whether you want to attract modern industrial development to your community starts and stops with available land. One of the lasting scars of the 2008–2011 Great Recession was the relative shutdown of bulk business park development, which delivered a supply of individual land sites to the market for resale to both developers and end users. Leading up to this time frame, developers were acquiring vast tracts of land to eventually put into production, often without having the delivery of the infrastructure figured out. In 2008, the land market hit the wall going 100 miles per hour, and financing alternatives effectively ceased overnight. The hangover for financial institutions lasted years, and the impact took down stalwart financial institutions such as Marshall & Ilsley bank.

As the market started to get back on its feet in 2011, land pricing was readjusted, balance sheets were cleaned up, and a new discipline emerged in land development. Owning land for the long haul was no longer a sound investment decision and suddenly was considered taboo. Land was needed only for the purpose of starting a defined construction project. Purchase contracts went from the "buy it and figure it out later" model to methodical due diligence periods in which a developer would not close on the deal until there was a guaranteed path to the development being approved. So why is this history lesson important? The changes that the Great Recession brought to the market have fundamentally altered how the private sector develops business parks.

SHOVEL READY

Wisconsin has a deep roster of small- to medium-sized privately held manufacturing enterprises that typically like to own their real estate. If you drive through several of the larger business parks located in the state, you will find many industrial buildings constructed in the mid-1980s through the late 1990s time frame. With the economy roaring, more and more communities welcomed the prospect of business park development to help bolster their industrial bases. Two of the most prolific business park developers in southeast Wisconsin during that time were WISPARK and MLG Commercial. The development model was primarily driven by a public and private partnership in which all infrastructure (such as streets, sewer, and water) were delivered by the community, and the developer finished the land and sold off lots one by one.

The system worked very well for the needs of the market at the time. Business park lots were generally five to ten acres in total size, which could typically accommodate a 25,000- to 150,000-square-foot building, the bread-and-butter of privately held industrial companies in Wisconsin. As noted earlier, a macrotrend emerged in the early 2000s that was going to fundamentally change the site and space needs of future business parks. Globalization was rapidly realigning the manufacturing footprint of industrial operations. The building boom of the prior fifteen-year period had provided ample domestic capacity, so future growth opportunities were being pursued in foreign markets. The demand for five- to ten-acre sites for small- to medium-sized manufacturers fell off the cliff, and the surge of business park development screeched to a halt.

The days of a single developer taking down several hundreds of acres of land and parceling off individual sites was over. The development costs and hold period had eroded all profit margins. A private sector developer simply no longer had a way to make money with this model.

Much of the business park land developed in this era was delivered with fixed infrastructure, such as interior roads. This practice unknowingly placed limitations on adapting to where the market was heading—buildings that were *big* and *bigger*, primarily driven by demand for logistics and warehouse space. I remember when Uline announced their first one-million-square-foot distribution center in Pleasant Prairie in 2010. I was scratching my head wondering how the company was going to fill up that single building. Ten years later and Uline's footprint in Kenosha County is five times that size, and it seems to be adding one million square feet every other year.

With private sector developers backing away from business park development, a shift in land development practice was needed. Development would be much more intentional and efficient. Infrastructure and roads would be planned around a specific use, not the other way around. To participate in the growth of the logistics and warehousing market, we were going to need access to an inventory of ready-to-build parcels that often exceeded fifteen acres, but the primary conduit of the past, the bulk land developer, was no longer in business. Developer-driven, build-to-suit, speculative development was going to be the new path of industrial development, with an occasional large end user surfacing in the market that could spark the development of a business park around its anchor use.

Without an assortment of shovel-ready parcels waiting in the wings for development, two significant challenges have emerged in keeping up with the growth of the industrial sector. The first is timing. An unimproved land site can take several months, if not years, to put into production. This eliminates fast-track site selection opportunities, which have become more and more common for end users. They simply do not have the time to wait for a site to become ready, so they move on to the next community (or state) who can fit their development timeline. The second challenge is that many manufacturing companies in Wisconsin prefer to own their real estate instead of lease. Developers have strategically pursued control and acquisition of the best-located industrial parcels and want the exact opposite outcome, long-term tenants who will lease the buildings. Much of the most desirable industrial land in key corridors runs through the control of a developer, which can eliminate a site from consideration if the end user will consider only ownership alternatives.

Is there another path to facilitate a more balanced delivery of industrial sites? Several communities like Beloit and Pleasant Prairie are leading the way with their own business parks. Successful business parks, such as the Gateway Business Park in Beloit and Prairie Highlands Corporate Park in Pleasant Prairie, were delivered by their respective communities to better control and manage the process of industrial development. The Haribo development in Pleasant Prairie is a prime example of a deal that likely would not have occurred without the community entering the domain of business park development. The well-known global giant, famous for its delicious gummy bears, was able to acquire the 136 acres of shovel-ready industrial land from the community that was needed to develop its $300-million North American production headquarters.[55] I predict that market forces will drive more and more communities into the business park development business, especially if the community is looking to attract manufacturing operations.

LAND...THEY AREN'T MAKING ANY MORE OF IT

Modern warehouses require land. And lots of it. The recent run-up in the value of industrial land has led to many more legacy farms coming into play for development projects. Large tracts of land, with quality access to population centers, are commanding record prices with multiple suitors. As a point of reference, only a decade ago, an unimproved parcel of land in metro Milwaukee might be able to command between $25,000 to $30,000 per acre. Fast-forward to 2022 and unimproved land is running five to six times that amount, approaching $140,000 per acre for the best sites. Ultimately, the costs get passed along to the end-business occupier. With limited supply, record demand, and skyrocketing development expenses, the expense of occupying industrial real estate is going up rapidly.

Kenosha County is a great example of how quickly key transportation corridors are changing. Over 1,000 acres of former agricultural land has been purchased or placed under option by prominent national industrial developers. They are banking on opportunities to lease space to the next big industrial business looking to expand in the market. The mad dash has led to more than seven million square feet of speculative buildings being planned in the Kenosha County market through the end of 2023. To put that number in perspective, about the same amount of square footage was built in the prior five-year period...in *total*.

Being close to Chicago presents a distinct advantage in attracting large-scale industrial development to areas like Kenosha. One of the primary hubs of distribution throughout the United States, the 1.3-billion-square-foot Chicago market is facing the same warehouse inventory challenges that led several larger users to consider Kenosha County. Many of these users need large-scale distribution centers that encompass up to one million square feet of space. While areas such as Kenosha and Rock County might attract the "Big Bomber" warehouse development of buildings that exceed 750,000 square feet, the demands of the e-commerce economy will drive the need for smaller fulfillment centers throughout the state. Because twenty-four-hour delivery has become the expectation, I believe Wisconsin will be a market in which localized fulfillment centers will proliferate across communities. Economic hubs such as Madison, the Fox Valley, Eau Claire, and Wausau are prime candidates for 25,000- to 100,000-square-foot, quick-turn fulfillment centers designed to service the delivery needs of the immediate trade area population base.

Just having available land will not be enough to attract most new industrial development. In my opinion, labor availability has vaulted past traditional site-selection drivers such as cost of occupancy and incentive offerings. Labor has become the most important box to check for site selection. One of the often-missed stories in the demise of big-box retail is the transitioning of the workforce from former department stores to fulfillment centers. Communities tend to view warehousing and fulfillment jobs as less glamorous than manufacturing, or even retail jobs, but warehousing is where the job growth is, especially for entry-level and lower-wage labor that would have been traditionally attracted to a retail store environment.

NATIONAL JOB GROWTH IN WAREHOUSING JOBS 2011-2021

FRED   All Employees Truck Transportation

Source: U.S. Bureau of Labor Statistics

Of course, finding the workforce remains priority number one. This challenge is particularly acute in rural areas of the state that do not have access to a dense population. The continued explosive growth in distribution and logistics will require a deep pool of manual labor, which will force many employers to locate near population centers. As a general rule of thumb, industrial development will typically attract ½ to 1 job per thousand square feet of space occupied in a distribution center environment and 1 to 1 ½ jobs in a manufacturing environment. Many new industrial developments will hold one hundred to three hundred jobs per building. I expect the employment-to-square-footage trend to continue to decrease over time, but we are a long way off from a fully automated environment. As employers battle it out to attract the best talent, communities can expect that companies will look to position themselves as a top place to work. Industrial companies are paying much more attention to the appearance and presentation of their facilities. Industrial real estate has come a long way from the grungy, billowing smokestack image of its past!

What can you do as a community if you are looking to grow your industrial base? Planning is an absolute necessity. Large-scale industrial developments can be rather complex, especially when accounting for infrastructure delivery. Typically, an unimproved site will consume between twelve to twenty-four months before a shovel is put in the ground. In addition to the planning, be prepared to discuss the impacts *and* economics with the constituents of your community. Yes, large-scale industrial development will create additional truck traffic; however, development is an economic boon for communities that can attract it. Industrial development creates job centers and an enormous amount of property tax revenue. As the Decade of Industrial brings manufacturing and supply chains back to the United States, and the e-commerce economy continues to reinvent how Americans shop, communities that sit on the sidelines will miss out on a key driving force of new economic development opportunity over the coming decade.

CHAPTER 10

ADAPT

> "It is not the strongest or most intelligent who will survive
> but those who can best manage change."
> —CHARLES DARWIN

SO FAR IN THIS BOOK I have provided actionable suggestions to allow Wisconsin's industrial companies to lead the way and flourish in our backyard over the coming decade. But what exactly does the future of Wisconsin's industrial base look like? Who are these companies I believe will lead the state into a new era of prosperity? Why are they located here? More importantly, what will lead them to invest more here?

How do we find out the answers to these questions? Let's ask one of them!

HUSCO: AN AMERICAN DREAM STORY

Husco is the type of company that makes up the core of Wisconsin industry. It is a privately held, family-owned business known as an innovative technology leader within its two industry verticals: hydraulic products for off-highway equipment manufacturers and electro-hydraulic and electro-mechanical components for automakers. Its customers include the likes of Caterpillar, John Deere, Ford, and General Motors. With 600 employees in Wisconsin and 1,500 around the world, Husco is part of a global supply chain and is thus exposed to many different macro perspectives shaping the future of the industrial economy.

Husco ended 2021 with a top line exceeding $500 million, and the CEO, Austin Ramirez, made public comments about doubling the size of the company to $1 billion within a five-year time frame. That's a bold statement not normally heard from a privately held family business in Wisconsin, but Austin is not your typical second-generation CEO either. He is widely recognized as one of Wisconsin's next-generation manufacturing thought leaders. In addition to his role as CEO of a global enterprise, he has already experienced the privilege of serving as a White House Fellow on the National Economic Council from 2016 to 2017. An honor of a lifetime, his service also opened his eyes to the difficulties of politically solving America's toughest challenges. Upon returning to the private sector, Austin was invited to join the boards of two of the premier manufacturing trade associations: National Association of Manufacturers (NAM) and National Equipment Manufacturers Association (NEMA). Did I mention that he is only in his early forties?

You might assume that Austin was a handpicked protégé for his current role dating back to his childhood, but he was not. His career path into the family business was never preordained. Austin completed his undergraduate at the University of Virginia with dual degrees in systems engineering and economics. He worked at McKinsey upon graduation. On his way to New York to take a job in finance, he received an unexpected call from his father, Gus, asking him to come back to Waukesha to join the family business. He had never considered it, and frankly never even spoke about it with his father, but something about the opportunity led him back home in 2003.

The Husco story is the quintessential American Dream. Husco was founded in Ohio in 1946 but quickly moved to open a new headquarters in Waukesha, Wisconsin, in 1947. In 1980, Husco was purchased by AMCA International. Austin's father, Gus Ramirez, joined AMCA in 1981 and was offered a position to lead the division shortly thereafter. Gus moved his family to the Waukesha area in 1982 for his new role, and in December of 1985 he orchestrated a highly leveraged buyout of the division. He became the proud owner of a business generating $15 million per year in revenue. Armed with advanced technologies and the freedom to pursue growth through untapped customers, Gus was able to rapidly build the business to $100 million in revenue by early 1992, just a few short years after betting it all. Husco is what Wisconsin's future in manufacturing needs to look like: a market leader with highly technical products that is entrepreneurial and profitable. The company is also unique in having grown organically from $15 million to over $500 million without a single acquisition.

I was able to interview Austin and discuss the role that Wisconsin can play in doubling the size of the company. While Wisconsin will remain Husco's home, scaling to $1 billion will be a global pursuit, and Austin predicts that up to 75 percent of new growth opportunities over the next five years will be outside the United States. Historically, this would have meant manufacturing products in plants located in Waukesha and Whitewater and exporting to other parts of the world, but the dual challenges of tariffs and the chaotic global supply chain have forced a pivot in its business model. With additional existing plants in India, China, and the UK, Husco was well positioned to transition into the "build and buy local" model, which has accelerated through the pandemic. Husco has embraced opportunities to both service and manufacture its products within distinct geographic markets, which has led to changes in its domestic operations.

With significant manufacturing being redirected to plants around the globe, Husco's US operations have shifted attention to maximizing performance in the two areas in which Austin believes America continues to lead the world: the technical and the sophisticated. As Husco grows market share around the globe, much of the company's strategy and innovation will continue to be developed out of its Wisconsin plants. While I note the impacts of more recent tariffs and supply chain challenges, the transformation of Husco has not been a reactive process. Starting with an epochal change in 2016, it offers an excellent case study in how to navigate the rapidly shifting landscape in manufacturing.

In addition to serving as global headquarters, the Waukesha facility was operated historically as a manufacturing plant for off-highway equipment. As 2016 approached, both of Husco's primary business units were presented with fork-in-the-road decisions. Off highway was becoming more and more driven by global customer demands that required committing resources to the local market being served. More opportunity to grow the business was on the horizon, but changes to its existing manufacturing practices were needed. The automotive business had an entirely different set of challenges; namely, electric vehicles (EVs). While likely more than a decade away, the wide-scale adoption to EVs ultimately could lead to the elimination of the primary products that Husco produces to support the internal combustion engines of gas-powered vehicles.

Husco needed decisive action. In 2016 it announced the shut-down and relocation of its off-highway lines from the Waukesha plant. This was not an end but a new beginning as it simultaneously committed to a $25-million investment to completely transform the facility to prepare for the next generation of automotive business.[56] Now more than five years into the decision, Austin reflects on the journey:

> Waukesha is the oldest plant in our footprint, but in many ways, it is the newest. We successfully retooled the entire plant to solely focus on opportunities that we are trying to capture in the automotive field. The investments have paid off. Automation has been able to significantly reduce direct labor, which has helped us manage the labor shortage. We are also winning market share with new product lines and generating more sales dollars per employee, which allows us to continue to reinvest in the business.

The performance of the company since the move has proven to be an unquestioned success, but there were many sleepless nights getting through to the other side. With a $25-million commitment on the line, Husco had to ask: why should we do this in Wisconsin? The ultimate answer was its people. Austin had a deep-seated belief that the state possessed both the breadth and depth of technical talent needed to grow the automotive business. Five years later, he continues to believe the technical talent available in Wisconsin is the state's single largest differentiator. "We have access to a deep bench of people who work hard, possess mechanical inclination, and know how to make things."

While Austin is a big believer in the capabilities of the state's industrial workforce, he also acknowledged a key concern of his that has been echoed several times throughout this book. Manufacturing has transitioned to a highly skilled career that needs advanced technical training. The good news is job candidates with strong work ethics and appropriate skillsets will experience unlimited demand for their services for years to come. The bad news is modern manufacturing has little room left for unskilled workers.

Our discussion turned to education, a top priority for the Ramirez family. Skilled labor requires education, and several of Wisconsin's most populated areas like Milwaukee and Racine continue to fall behind in K–12 results. "The postsecondary system in Wisconsin is hands down one of the best in the world, but I have grave concerns that the K–12 foundation is crumbling. Action is needed here, or we will reach a tipping point over the next decade where our deep bench becomes empty."

Austin has particular interest in improving education outcomes in the Milwaukee area, and his passion extends beyond paying lip service. In 2017, the Ramirez Family Foundation opened St. Augustine Preparatory, a K–12 choice school on the south side of Milwaukee. Currently serving 1,350 students, the school boasts a 96.1 percent attendance rate and was recognized recently as the number-one-rated K–12 school in the state by the Department of Education.[57] As a point of comparison, the Milwaukee Public School system reports an attendance rate of 86.3 percent and graduates only 67.4 percent of its students within four years.[58] Also, Austin is not afraid to confront the status quo that so often permeates the educational system.

Racial disparity in education outcomes is a huge problem for the state. The performance standards of MPS compared to its suburban peers consistently produces one of the largest achievement gaps throughout the United States. When we talk about workforce challenges and the need for skilled labor, we cannot accept the fact that the largest school system in the state of Wisconsin is being left behind. Education is the number one issue facing Wisconsin's competitiveness.

So, what needs to happen to better improve the business climate in the state of Wisconsin? Not surprising, when I asked Austin what were the two most impactful actions he would take if he were governor for the day, fixing education was his immediate response. "We need to address the broken system of our K–12 funding models. Transparency of results is lacking, and there needs to be an equitable system for how public, charter, and choice schools are funded. Results need to matter." Because of his experience at the National Economic Council, his second priority would be to implement Final Five Voting for Wisconsin's state and federal elections. The current political environment has effectively taken bipartisan compromise off the table. Austin cited Alaska recently implementing this new voting system and several other states running active ballot initiatives to implement a system that rewards politicians for achieving results instead of pandering to partisan extremes.[59]

We concluded our conversation with Austin's vision of Wisconsin 2030. "I believe in Wisconsin, and I believe that private-sector employers are figuring out how to not only survive but thrive in the new world. Will it be challenging? Absolutely. But we have the talent right here that can get it done."

OLD BECOMES NEW AGAIN

Husco is just one example of many companies located throughout Wisconsin that fly under the radar but make a tremendous impact at the local level. Take Green Bay Packaging, a privately held, eighty-five-year-old business headquartered in the city from which the company name is derived. It is an industry leader in innovative packaging solutions and occupies thirty-seven facilities across the United States. Green Bay Packaging could choose to invest anywhere, but when it came time to build a state-of-the-art paper mill, the single largest investment in the history of the company, it doubled down on the state of Wisconsin. The $500-million project preserved 1,100 jobs in the Green Bay area and will ultimately create 1,500 throughout the state.[60]

Paper mills built communities throughout Wisconsin in the twentieth century, so a paper mill is one of the first things that comes to my mind when I think of "old" industry. But many new lines of business are growing in paper and packaging products, and Green Bay Packaging will be on the cutting edge of the next generation of those business opportunities. The mill will provide an anchor in the Fox Valley and build the twenty-first century version of paper expertise in the state.

Saputo Cheese, a leading global cheese brand and one of the top three producers in the United States, is another good example. It has a significant legacy footprint throughout the state of Wisconsin and in 2022 started construction of an $85-million plant in the community of Franklin. The facility is a big bet on its future; it could have placed the facility anywhere, yet it picked Wisconsin. The project will support 650 jobs, and the attractiveness of the labor pool in the Milwaukee area was a primary driver for the site selection.[61] This was a big win for the state and, in my opinion, a *must* win. For many residents of Wisconsin, cheese is its own food group, outside of dairy! It is also another "old" industry that is attracting new investment. Cheeseheads across the state can be proud to know that their favorite Saputo Cheese products will be made here for decades to come.

These are the types of companies that make up a large swath of Wisconsin's economy. You might not immediately recognize their names, but they most certainly lead their markets and lead their communities. We can not only keep them here, but we can grow them here. All we need to do is continue to adapt.

2030

"There are risks and costs to action. But they are far less
than the long-range risks of comfortable inaction."
—**PRESIDENT JOHN F. KENNEDY**

WHAT DO WE WANT WISCONSIN to look like when 2030 hits the calendar? Do we want the state to be a vibrant engine of economic growth and opportunity? What will success look like? Let's venture several years into the future and take a look.

January 1, 2030: The Decade of Industrial has delivered great change to the state of Wisconsin. The last of the baby boomer generation is now over sixty-five years old, and our industrial workforce has officially turned over. While a tremendous amount of human talent has moved into retirement, we have been able to continue to grow our industrial output throughout the decade by more than 30 percent. We have accomplished this by rebuilding a smaller, nimbler workforce who has developed the skillset to continue the advancement of products and processes that represent the technical and the sophisticated. Companies throughout the state have complete confidence in their ability to place large capital investments in plants and equipment. We have successfully cultivated an environment in which business leaders know we have developed both the human capital and technological capital that will allow for them to excel in growing their businesses right here in Wisconsin.

When January 1, 2030, arrives, the above paragraph represents a vision that I would define as *mission accomplished*. We have some choices to make as we move through the next decade. If we do nothing, the wave of retirees and population stagnation inevitably will place many of our industrial employers in a position in which they will not be able to find the required talent they need to grow in the state of Wisconsin. They will be forced to look elsewhere.

I began this book reviewing the Foxconn project and the grand ambitions of Wisconn Valley. For many of the initial supporters of the project, including me, Wisconn Valley represented an instantaneous opportunity to transition our economy into what we believed our future called for. It was an opportunity to change the economic prospects of the state in one fell swoop. Perhaps, we had developed an unspoken yet deep-seated belief that we couldn't do this on our own. We needed outside influence. In a way, I believe Foxconn represented the allure of the easy button.

Although the project has not come close to performing as it was initially drawn up, I believe we have learned many lessons that might not be obvious unless we are looking for them. I believe Foxconn forced an introspective review of what our economic future looks like and, maybe more importantly, what it does *not* look like. The future of Wisconsin's industry needs to look very much like what Foxconn, as a figurehead, wanted to achieve on its own: a dominant manufacturing hub that leads the world in advanced technologies and attracts the best and brightest talent to live, work, and play right here in Wisconsin. If you look beyond all the negativity associated with the project, you will see what I believe is the path forward. It was right in front of us all along. The path forward will be forged by the many great people and businesses that already call Wisconsin home. These companies are industry leaders already located here, companies I profiled throughout this book, like Milwaukee Tool, Generac, and Husco. These are the types of companies that were built here and want to grow here. We must provide them with the environment they need to get it done.

If we want to remain a top-tier industrial state, how are we going to get there? We know that we are facing an industrial worker shortage. We have learned that we are slowly but surely changing the narrative for industrial careers. We know where we are having success, and we also know that to get to the next level, we will need industry, education, government, and parents to all row in the same direction. Even if we are successful in bringing more people into industrial careers, we will need to be a leader in automating our processes through the use of technology and robotics. To remain industry leaders, our manufacturers must be pioneers in delivering the promises of Industry 4.0. As we grow our workforce, we need to provide affordable workforce housing solutions. This is a key lifestyle amenity for the middle class, and Wisconsin must be known as a national destination in which residents can affordably raise their families. Business in the twenty-first century requires uninterrupted connectivity and access to world-class infra-structure. We need to ensure that our existing infrastructure remains in top-tier condition and that our new investments in areas such as broadband address the needs of the future. Economic development pursuits will still require the use of incentives, and we need to ensure that Wisconsin is playing to its strengths. Our offerings must include more alternatives to incentivize small- and medium-sized businesses. With our industrial base primed to grow in the state, we will need to make sure that they have access to the real estate they will need to build and occupy new facilities.

The path forward is not complicated, but it's not easy. Business as usual is comfortable. It's what we know. Several of these areas will require changes to societal norms that we have come to accept, and changing public perception can be the most difficult type of change to achieve. So where do you start?

If you are a business owner or executive, you must under-stand that it is no longer good enough to only talk about your workforce challenges. Getting in the game must be part of your long-term strategic plan. Get involved with business associa-tions and chambers of commerce that are focused on work-force development. Work with your local schools and colleges and show them what you are doing in your business. Commu-nicate with your local representatives on key pieces of legisla-tion that can help you achieve your goals.

If you are an elected official, you must understand that the pace of business is only accelerating. The businesses in your community need solutions, and they are in need of decisive action. While businesses understand election cycles, they also cannot sit on their hands and wait for an election to pass. Reach out to the businesses in your community and try to engage in a conversation. It amazes me that in this age of connection, still very few thoughtful discussions occur between policy leaders and business leaders.

If you are a parent, have an open mind to your child pursuing a path that might not include a four-year degree. Learn about what is occurring in modern industry and talk to your child about the earning potential.

If you are an employee trying to build your American Dream, let your local community planner know that your community needs more affordable workforce housing. Talk to your neighbors that might be against new development and let them know what it means to be able to plant your family roots with a new home.

2030 is not that far away. Let's build on our foundation and get to work.

ACKNOWLEDGMENTS

PULLING THIS BOOK TOGETHER was the result of a personal journey that I went through in 2020.

I want to thank my father, Dennis Hoffman (1951–2020), who passed away on January 23, 2020, for showing me the path for how to get to this moment. My mother, Nancy, has been a rock for our family and without her guidance, my life would most certainly be much different. The grieving process that I went through in 2020 led me to the next phase in life.

I entered the Strategic Coach program in November of 2020 and I would not have been able to pull together the concept, or the team, to create a book without the vision that Strategic Coach has brought to my life. Dan Sullivan is the founder of Strategic Coach and a prolific author. I tuned into a Zoom call in spring of 2021 with Dan and Tucker Max that covered the *why* and *how* to write a book. My interest was piqued, which led me to Scribe Media. Scribe has been an incredible partner to work with and I would highly recommend them for anyone looking to write a book.

The project really started to take form when Suzanne Kelley agreed to my request to be interviewed. Without Suzanne,

I would not have taken the next steps to approach Rich Barnhouse, Kent Lorenz, Matt Neumann, and Austin Ramirez. I want to thank all of them for sharing their perspectives. Their insights really pulled the book together. My father-in-law David Alpert has provided me with an excellent sounding board over the course of my career and he provided a big lift for me in formulating the content on broadband. I want to thank Tracy Johnson at CARW, Jim Villa at NAIOP, Steve Kohlmann at IBAW, Mike Theo and Tom Larson at the WRA, and Suzanne Kelley (once again) and her incredible staff at the WCBA. I have had the honor to serve on the boards of all these great organizations and without those opportunities, this book would not have been possible. I would also like to thank all the board members of these organizations that I have served with over the years.

I want to thank my business partners and teammates, specifically Chad Vande Zande, Nick Unger, Caitlin Wilde, and Gao Moua. The work that we do day in and day out provided the passion for me to undertake the journey of writing this book.

Finally, I want to thank my wife, Amanda. You let me be me as I crafted this project and didn't ask questions or share any doubts. I hope the finished product is helpful in creating a future Wisconsin that we can enjoy with our children, Gavin and Malayna.

ENDNOTES

1. Shawn Johnson, "Wisconsin Fell Short of 250k Job Goal during Walker's 8 Years in Office," Wisconsin Public Radio, June 6, 2019, https://www.wpr.org/wisconsin-fell-short-250k-job-goal-during-walkers-8-years-office.

2. Nusaiba Mizan, "Fact-Check: Did Scott Walker's Policies Grow Wisconsin's Manufacturing Sector?" *Green Bay Press-Gazette*, October 29, 2019, https://www.greenbaypressgazette.com/story/money/2019/10/29/did-former-governor-scott-walkers-policies-grow-wisconsins-manufacturing-sector/3989007002/.

3. Yoko Kubota, "Taiwan's Foxconn Eyes Seven States for $10 Billion Investment," *Wall Street Journal*, June 22, 2017, https://www.wsj.com/articles/foxconn-in-talks-with-u-s-states-over-new-plant-1498105489.

4. Nancy Crotti, "Medtronic, Foxconn Aim to Make 10,000 Ventilators," Medical Design and Outsourcing, June 18, 2020, https://www.medicaldesignandoutsourcing.com/medtronic-foxconn-aim-to-make-10000-ventilators/.

5. Mark Kass, "Milwaukee Tool's Steve Richman Named 2021 Executive of the Year," *Milwaukee Business Journal*, November 18, 2021, https://www.bizjournals.com/milwaukee/news/2021/11/18/milwaukee-tools-steve-richman.html.

6. Dave Umhoefer, "Scott Walker Says His 250,000 Jobs Promise Was a 'Big Goal,'" Politifact, October 30, 2014, https://www.politifact.com/factchecks/2014/oct/30/scott-walker/scott-walker-says-his-250000-jobs-promise-was-big-/.

7. US Census Bureau, "Wisconsin Population Increased 3.6% since 2010," The United States Census Bureau, October 8, 2021, https://www.census.gov/library/stories/state-by-state/wisconsin-population-change-between-census-decade.html.

8. Christina Farr, "EPIC Systems Says Employees Can Now Work from Home until the End of the Year after Attempt to Get Them to Return This Month," CNBC, August 13, 2020, https://www.cnbc.com/2020/08/13/epic-systems-says-employees-can-now-work-from-home-until-the-end-of-the-year.html.

9. "Home," Wisconsin Technical College System, accessed March 14, 2022, https://www.wtcsystem.edu/.

10. Waukesha County Technical College, *Impact*, Spring 2022, 6, https://www.wctc.edu/_site-pdfs/wctc-impact-spring-2022.pdf.

11. "WISH: Annual Number of Wisconsin Births, 1990–2020," Wisconsin Department of Health Services, September 28, 2021, https://www.dhs.wisconsin.gov/wish/birth/data.htm.

12. Waukesha County Technical College, *Graduate Success 2019* (Pewaukee: WCTC, 2019), accessed March 15, 2022, https://www.wctc.edu/_site-pdfs/graduate-success-reports/graduate-success-2019.pdf.

13. Jason Stein, Mark Sommerhauser, and Muhammad Shayan, *Falling Behind? The State of Wisconsin's Public Universities and Colleges* (Milwaukee: Wisconsin Policy Forum, 2020), 28, https://wispolicyforum.org/wp-content/uploads/2020/12/FallingBehind_FullReport-compressed.pdf.

14. Sharada Dharmasankar and Bhash Mazumder, "Have Borrowers Recovered from Foreclosures during the Great Recession?" Federal Reserve Bank of Chicago, 2016, https://www.chicagofed.org/publications/chicago-fed-letter/2016/370.

15. Evan Cunningham, "Great Recession, Great Recovery? Trends from the Current Population Survey," *Monthly Labor Review*, U.S. Bureau of Labor Statistics, April 2018, https://www.bls.gov/opub/mlr/2018/article/great-recession-great-recovery.htm.

16. Robert Atkinson, "Why the 2000s Were a Lost Decade for American Manufacturing," *Industry Week*, March 14, 2013, https://www.industryweek.com/the-economy/article/22006840/why-the-2000s-were-a-lost-decade-for-american-manufacturing.

17. Dan Burns and Howard Schneider, "US Employment in the 2010s in Five Charts," Reuters, January 10, 2020, https://www.reuters.com/article/us-usa-economy-jobs-graphic/u-s-employment-in-the-2010s-in-five-charts-idUSKBN1Z92AK.

18. Melissa S. Kearney and Phillip B. Levine, "Will Births in the US Rebound? Probably Not.," Brookings, May 24, 2021, https://www.brookings.edu/blog/up-front/2021/05/24/will-births-in-the-us-rebound-probably-not/#:~:text=Recently%20released%20official%20U.S.%20birth,2007%2C%20a%2020%20percent%20decline.

19. James Causey, "Lack of jobs continues to haunt city's turnaround efforts," Journal Sentinel , April 27,2017, https://projects.jsonline.com/news/2017/4/27/lack-of-jobs-continues-to-haunt-citys-turnaround-efforts.html

20. "Wisconsin Alumni Research Foundation," WARF, March 14, 2022, https://www.warf.org/.

21. "Home Page," C-Motive, accessed February 1, 2022, https://www.c-motive.com/.

22. "Wisconsin Housing Statistics," Wisconsin REALTORS Association, March 26,2022, https://www.wra.org/HousingStatistics/.

23. "September 2021 Home Sales Report," Wisconsin REALTORS Association, October 18, 2021, https://www.wra.org/HSRSep2021/.

24. "Housing Data," Wisconsin Builders Association, February 28, 2022, https://www.wisbuild.org/housing-data.

25. "September 2021 Home Sales Report."

26. Michael B. Sauter, "Income It Takes to Be Considered Middle Class in Every State," 24/7 Wall St., November 10, 2020, https://247wallst.com/special-report/2020/11/10/income-it-takes-to-be-considered-middle-class-in-every-state-2/.

27. Erica Pennington, "Amazon Site Plans Given the All-Clear in Beloit," *Beloit Daily News*, last revised January 20, 2020, https://www.beloitdailynews.com/statelinebusiness/news/amazon-site-plans-given-the-all-clear-in-beloit/article_9236e186-9951-510d-8b03-e80212a91e4c.html.

28. Wisconsin Department of Revenue, *Tax Incremental Financing Manual* (Milwaukee: Department of Revenue, 2022), 22, https://www.revenue.wi.gov/DOR%20Publications/tif-manual.pdf.

29. Curt Witynski, "Using TIF to Benefit Affordable Housing," *The Municipality*, January 2018, https://www.lwm-info.org/DocumentCenter/View/1926/Using-TIF-to-Benefit-Affordable-Housing?bidId=.

30. Infrastructure Investment and Jobs Act of 2021, Pub. L. No. 117-58, 135 Stat. 429 (2021), https://www.congress.gov/117/plaws/publ58/PLAW-117publ58.pdf.

31. ASCE Wisconsin Section, *Wisconsin 2020 Infrastructure Report Card* (Milwaukee: Wisconsin Section of the American Society of Civil Engineers, 2021), 5, https://infrastructurereportcard.org/wp-content/uploads/2020/09/FullReport-WI_2020-1.pdf.

32. Alex Moe, "Wisconsin to Get Billions in Federal Dollars through Infrastructure Bill," WisBusiness, November 9, 2021, https://www.wisbusiness.com/2021/wisconsin-to-get-billions-in-federal-dollars-through-infrastructure-bill/.

33. "I-94 East–West Corridor Study, Milwaukee—Milwaukee County," Wisconsin Department of Transportation, February 15, 2022, https://wisconsindot.gov/Pages/projects/by-region/se/94stadiumint/default.aspx.

34. Alex Zank, "Proposed Alternative to I-94 East–West Expansion Gets Pushback from Business Groups," BizTimes, September 17, 2021, https://biztimes.com/proposed-alternative-to-i-94-east-west-expansion-gets-pushback-from-business-groups/.

35. Wisconsin Department of Transportation, 2020–2021 *Transportation Budget Trends* (Madison: Wisconsin Department of Transportation, 2021), 5–6, https://wisconsindot.gov/Documents/about-wisdot/performance/budget/TransportationBudgetTrends2020-21.pdf.

36. Gretchenn DuBois and Kevin Pula, "Recent Legislative Actions Likely to Change Gas Taxes," National Conference of State Legislatures, August 10, 2021, https://www.ncsl.org/research/transportation/2013-and-2014-legislative-actions-likely-to-change-gas-taxes.aspx.

37. Joe Peterangelo, Virginia Carlson, and Rob Henken, *Getting to Work: Opportunities and Obstacles to Improving Transit Service to Suburban Milwaukee Job Hubs* (Milwaukee: Public Policy Forum, 2013), 12, https://wispolicyforum.org/wp-content/uploads/2019/05/GettingToWork.pdf.

38. Molly Collins, "$13.5 Million Transportation Victory," ACLU of Wisconsin, April 16, 2018, https://www.aclu-wi.org/en/news/135-million-transportation-victory.

39. Patrick Leary, "JobLines Bus Service Continues, Temporarily, with Milwaukee County Funding," *Milwaukee Business Journal*, January 8, 2019, https://www.bizjournals.com/milwaukee/news/2019/01/09/joblines-bus-service-continues-temporarily-with.html.

40. "FCC Annual Broadband Deployment Report Shows Digital Divide Is Rapidly Closing," Federal Communications Commission, April 5, 2021, https://www.fcc.gov/document/fcc-annual-broadband-report-shows-digital-divide-rapidly-closing.

41. "Biennial Budget," Wisconsin State Legislature, 2021 - 2023 , https://docs.legis.wisconsin.gov/misc/lfb/budget.

42. Danielle Kaeding, "Wisconsin Makes $100m Available for Broadband Expansion and More Federal Money Is on the Way," Wisconsin Public Radio, November 10, 2021, https://www.wpr.org/wisconsin-makes-100m-available-broadband-expansion-and-more-federal-money-way.

43. Governor's Task Force on Broadband Access, *Report to Governor Tony Evers and Wisconsin State Legislature* (Madison: Public Service Commission of Wisconsin, 2021), https://psc.wi.gov/Documents/broadband/2021%20Governors%20Task%20Force%20on%20Broadband%20Access.pdf.

44. "Electricity Costs by State," Quick Electricity, accessed February 18, 2022, https://quickelectricity.com/average-electricity-prices-and-deregulation/.

45. "Electric Power Monthly," U.S. Energy Information Administration, April 2022, https://www.eia.gov/electricity/monthly/epm_table_grapher.php?t=epmt_5_06_a.

46. Arthur Thomas, "Foxconn Electricity Needs Require $140 Million in Upgrades, ATC Says," BizTimes, July 3, 2019, https://biztimes.com/foxconn-electricity-needs-require-140-million-in-upgrades-atc-says/.

47. "About Us," Wisconsin Industrial Energy Group, accessed January 24, 2022, https://wieg.org/about-us/.

48. FoxBusiness.com, "Wisconsin Wasn't Highest Bidder for Foxconn Plant, Gov. Walker Says," Yahoo! Finance, August 1, 2017, https://finance.yahoo.com/news/wisconsin-wasn-apos-t-highest-171400687.html.

49. Carrie Ghose and Eleanor Kennedy, "Ohio Reveals Incentive Package That Landed Intel Plant Sought by Wisconsin," *Milwaukee Business Journal*, January 28, 2022, https://www.bizjournals.com/milwaukee/news/2022/01/28/heres-what-ohio-is-offering-intel.html.

50. NAIOP Wisconsin Chapter, Commercial Real Estate Development Association, and Wisconsin Realtors Association, *Tax Increment Financing: An Analysis of Wisconsin's Most Important Economic Development Tool* (Madison: Baker Tilly, 2019), 4, https://aaaed961-2523-4efa-9c25-1d9686d120b4.filesusr.com/ugd/629139_64e9b8c0b4d44f0d84e4fe406eca06a3.pdf.

51. "Memorandum of Understanding between Racine County, and Community Care, Inc.," Racine County, 2007, https://www.racinecounty.com/Home/ShowDocument?id=10539.

52. "Wisconsin Economic Development Corporation Program Guidelines for Fiscal Year 2020," Wisconsin Economic Development Corporation, 2020, https://wedc.org/wp-content/uploads/2020/01/BCD_BTC_FY20_AAC _clean_R1.pdf.

53. Katie Gremban, "Marketbeat Milwaukee Industrial Q1 2022," Cushman & Wakefield, April 13, 2022, https://www.cushmanwakefield.com/en/united-states/insights/us-marketbeats/milwaukee-marketbeats.

54. Craig Meyer and Rich Thompson, "Industrial Real Estate Demand on the Rise in the US," JLL, July 8, 2020, https://www.us.jll.com/en/views/industrial -real-estate-demand-on-the-rise-in-the-us.

55. Vincent Ryan, "HARIBO of America CFO Plans for Gummies Growth," CFO, March 29, 2021, https://www.cfo.com/corporate-finance/2021/03/haribo-of-america-cfo-plans-for-gummies-growth-4539/.

56. Arthur Thomas, "Husco to End off-Highway Production in Waukesha," BizTimes, June 30, 2016, https://biztimes.com/husco-to-end-off-highway -production-in-waukesha/.

57. "Home," Augustine Prep, January 27, 2022, http://www.augprep.org/.

58. Milwaukee Public Schools, *2022–23 Superintendent's Proposed Budget: Informational Section* (Milwaukee: Milwaukee Public Schools), 4B-8, 4B-16, accessed March 15, 2022, https://mps.milwaukee.k12.wi.us/MPS-English/CFO/Budget--Finance/Informational.pdf.

59. "Final-Five Voting," The Institute for Political Innovation, December 17, 2021, https://political-innovation.org/final-five-voting/.

60. "Green Bay Packaging New Recycled Paper Mill Begins Production," Green Bay Packaging, March 19, 2021, https://gbp.com/corrugated-packaging/newsroom/green-bay-packaging-new-recycled-paper-mill-begins-production.

61. TM4J Web Staff, "A Proposed Cheese Packing Plant Could Bring 650 Jobs to Franklin," TMJ4, January 11, 2022, https://www.tmj4.com/news/local-news/a-proposed-cheese-packing-plant-could-bring-650-jobs-to-franklin.